NOT BY MIGHT, NOR BY POWER

Mildred Eine,
    Praise the Lord for
evidence that He's still
doing mighty things if we
let Him!
        — Joyce Metzler Baker

NOT BY MIGHT, NOR BY POWER

Story of the Paul Metzlers, 47-year
Missionaries to the Heart of Africa

Joyce Metzler Baker

REGULAR BAPTIST PRESS
1300 North Meacham Road
Schaumburg, Illinois 60173–4888

Library of Congress Cataloging-in-Publication Data

Baker, Joyce Metzler, 1957–
Not by might, nor by power: story of the Paul Metzlers, 47-year
missionaries to the heart of Africa/Joyce Metzler Baker.
p. cm.
ISBN 0–87227–135–8
1. Metzler, Paul, 1902–1969. 2. Metzler, Etiennette. 3. Metzler, Hélène,
d. 1967. 4. Missionaries—Chad—Biography.
5. Missionaries—United States—Biography. 6. Baptists—Biography.
7. Metzler family. I. Title.
BV3625.C47B35   1989
266'.61' 0922—dc20

[B] 89–27002
CIP

NOT BY MIGHT, NOR BY POWER
© 1990
Regular Baptist Press
Schaumburg, Illinois

Not by might, nor by power, but by my spirit, saith the Lord of hosts.

Zechariah 4:6

Dedication

Lovingly dedicated to Etiennette Metzler
Mother and Grandmother

CONTENTS

Acknowledgments

Hélène Metzler was a veteran missionary-nurse by 1966 when she first became ill. The symptoms seemed to indicate a tapeworm. She had treated this condition so many times in others that she knew just what medicine to take. She kept working in the dispensary in Africa and soon felt great again.

The symptoms returned later, but this time they did not respond as quickly to the same treatment. Hélène stubbornly refused to let her own discomforts get in the way when she could be helping to ease some pain and suffering among her beloved Chadians. Besides, she would probably start feeling better any day.

She never did start feeling better, and in fact became extremely ill. Finally she realized she had to go to Koumra to see Dr. Dave Seymour, another second-generation missionary. He sent her right out, explaining that diagnostic techniques and equipment in the United States far surpassed what he had in the heart of Africa.

Doctors at the Baptist Mid-Missions home office in Cleveland diagnosed cancer and operated immediately. They reported that they had successfully removed the tumor but did not tell their nurse-patient that her disease had metastasized. Among themselves they gave her eighteen months to live. The Lord gave her nineteen.

Dr. Jon Rouch, who had been field medical director for Chad and the Central African Republic before becoming the Mission medical director, contacted Paul and Etiennette to say Hélène could now go home. They had been forced back to the States from Chad again because of Paul's back problems, and were in the middle of meetings in Miami as field representatives for the Mission. They took their oldest child to their home to rest.

Even as a youngster, Hélène had dreamed of writing a book "someday," and this forced furlough seemed like a good time to start. She chose subjects from her life and experience for her prose as she had for her poetry. Besides scouring her own memory, she cornered her parents as often as she could for details in order to put together the original manuscript for this biography.

"Many thanks are due to my sister-in-law, Mrs. Jack Metzler, and to Mrs. Karl E. Gwin for giving of their time and their energy in the typing of the manuscript," she put on the original acknowledgment.

She planned to polish her work as she felt better, and to find a publisher for it eventually. Before too many months, however, her nurse's mind realized she would not be able to play out her dream to

9

be published after all. She would not recover and return to Chad either. There would not be time.

"We know this is part of the development of the illness," she said when something new especially bothered one of her parents. "The Lord will give us grace to handle it."

Hélène was terribly disappointed that she would not see her dear friends in Chad again, but she knew she would see the Christians one day in Heaven. Glorious Heaven. Where Jesus waited for her.

She wrote in a prayer letter:

Home at Last

I didn't know, when the Lord said no to returning to Africa, that He would say yes to going Home so soon. However, my heart is filled with joy as I anticipate it, and my mind is constantly filled with thoughts of the many happy reunions I shall soon be having with loved ones and—best of all—my Savior! How wonderful that the Lord is going to give me such a glorious reward so soon. I do not feel that I deserve it already when I have done so little for Him—but I'm leaving that up to my Lord.

Of course, I have no idea how soon I'll be going; but if I am still here in September, I will write again. If not, my mother has promised to write and let you know. . . .

For anyone who should happen to want to send flowers after I have left this world, I would appreciate it much more if you would send money instead. That will be put in the Chad translation fund. Thank you.

She asked that she not be put on life support systems when the time came. Why put off life with her Savior?

On November 17, 1967, Hélène Metzler left the pain of a cancer-ridden body for the exhilaration of a glorified body in Heaven with her Lord.

* * *

My mother, Lois Harshman Metzler, became friends with Aunt Hélène in nursing school before getting to know her brother Edwin.

"Hélène spent her whole life preparing for or working on the mission field," Mother has said while sharing her warm memories.

I remember visiting my aunt during Christmas vacation in 1966. My parents knew this might be the last time they could bring the family down to see her.

My child's mind understood something was seriously wrong with Aunt Hélène since grown-ups spoke about her quietly with their heads huddled together, but I could not figure out what it was. She was thin underneath her ample robe and fuzzy slippers, and she spent a good deal of time in an easy chair, but she laughed a lot. She teased Dad just as mercilessly as he teased her, and often found something to laugh about in everyday life.

"And the nurse said she'd hold my stomach while I coughed," she told us one day with a chuckle, "but I said 'Thank you, but why don't I hold my own stomach and let you cough.' "

She even came outside to sit by the lake when Grandpa took us kids fishing. Her contented smile is in the snapshot she gave me.

In late 1981, Grandma Metzler and Aunt Evelyne asked if I would like to prepare the manuscript for publication. I jumped at the chance before realizing I did not know how Aunt Hélène would have wanted it done. So I prayed for wisdom and plunged in, adding my own research to fill in gaps and provide historical background, and tailoring the manuscript for a more recent readership.

Throughout the book I have stayed as close to actual facts and events as possible, using Aunt Hélène's information, letters from Grandma (Etiennette) and Grandpa (Paul), and the memories of several family members. I claimed literary license only in order to bring out personalities that may have been obscured otherwise, or to add emphasis to what really happened.

Despite chronic back trouble and periodic illness, Grandma checked and rechecked my last few revisions to help maintain accuracy and to add accent marks to all the foreign words. She patiently answered my long letters full of questions and dug out irreplaceable pictures of the family and the work.

I would like to thank Grandma, my aunts, my parents and my husband for their faith in me, their encouragement and prayers and their input. My sisters and friends added their encouragement, and my husband Gary showed special support by not complaining when dinner was late and by buying me a Kaypro to speed things up.

Mrs. Alys Chapin, former English instructor at Spurgeon Baptist Bible College, helped Grandma go over my revision, and Ellen Reed, a friend of the family, made herself available to help Grandma with the picture project, communication and more.

Special thanks goes to two instructors from the Maranatha Christian Writers' Conference: Dick Bohrer, professor of journalism at Liberty University, for his suggestions for the manuscript; and Jack Metzler (not related), author, for his encouragement and suggestions for the project.

I also would like to thank Mrs. Ann Craglione from Regular Baptist Press who, although missionary biographies are often not the most popular genre among publishers, believed in this one and started the ball rolling.

Joyce Metzler Baker

Letter to the Reader

A letter to the reader from Paul Metzler before his death:

For many years Christian friends have urged me to put into book form the account of our experiences as we have served our Lord as missionaries. Lest some think that we have sought self-glorification, I have hesitated to write a book. However, to satisfy the desire of our daughter Hélène, we give the accounts written in this book.

This is not an exhaustive biography. Much more could be added to give glory to our wonderful Lord for His leading and gracious provision for our needs, despite our continual mistakes and failings. God has been gracious in allowing us to share with the other missionaries of Baptist Mid-Missions the work of giving the gospel to the people of the Central African Republic and the Republic of Chad. He has surely shown us that His strength is manifested through our weakness. To Him be the glory!

Photos

The photos, furnished by Baptist Mid-Missions, the author and other family members, are gratefully acknowledged.

CHAPTER
1

The Lord nurtures Paul as he grows up, and He leads him to Moody.

T
he *S.S. Thysville,* flying the Belgian flag, left France behind and lumbered toward French Equatorial Africa.

"Yes, I understand this is the ship's maiden voyage," twenty-one-year-old Paul Fred Metzler commented to his companion. "Now I've, on the other hand, come across the Atlantic already." He tucked his thumbs under the seam of his sleeves and strutted a bit. "Guess I'm a seasoned salt by now."

He could not stop the chuckle that bubbled in his throat. It spilled out and drew in his companion.

"You're in a good mood," his friend said laughing. "Are you starting an extended holiday?"

"Oh no," Paul replied, rubbing his eye. "I'm a missionary under the General Council of Cooperating Baptist Missions of North America, Incorporated. We call it the Mid-Africa Mission for short. Guess 'missionary' is supposed to mean 'staid and proper,' but right now I feel mighty free."

"Yeah? What's up?"

Paul became a bit dreamy.

"I just left my fiancée. What a gal! She'll be following. . . ."

"Hey!" called a knot of young people. "There you are. Come and get in these pictures."

He will never miss me, Paul's companion thought with a smile and hurried off.

Paul leaned against the railing and let the restless waves cast their spell on him. They buoyed his thoughts away, back over the ways in which the Lord had led in his life.

The oldest in a family of five boys, Paul grew up in the small town of Mishawaka, Indiana. He especially remembered the many good times spent at Grandma Metzler's house just down the road. Every Sunday morning she would make sure the boys had had breakfast and were dressed, and off she would go to Sunday School and church with five little escorts.

Paul dutifully set an example for his younger brothers by learning his Sunday School lessons. Oh, how he remembered struggling to keep the Ten Commandments in order! The Beatitudes often defied the boy's memory, but those books of the Bible were nearly impossible even to pronounce.

"Say it again, Paul," one pal taunted.

"Yeah, say 'Nehemiah,' " another giggled.

"S-say it yours-self," Paul shot back, his face getting warm.

"Oh come on," they pressed. "Try 'Leviticus.' "

"T-try this," Paul hissed and let loose a clenched fist.

15

"Boys! Boys! Stop that!" the Sunday School teacher cried. "There'll be no fighting in God's house."

Paul just never could bring himself to turn the other cheek when anyone teased him about his speech impediment. Despite this deviation in practical theology, he was baptized and joined the church at twelve years of age.

By this time the Lord had begun to teach the boy ambition and perseverance. He got up early each morning for four years to sell newspapers on the street corners across town in order to buy most of his own clothes. At fourteen, he dropped out of eighth grade because his father had become too sick to work. He settled into one of the many vacancies in mechanical work at Bendix (now Uniroyal). The workers kept leaving to fight for their country in World War I.

Paul thrilled to news of the war efforts. His job seemed dull in comparison, so as soon as he turned seventeen he tried to enlist.

"No, you're not going off to war," his father declared. "We need you here. Besides, you're just a boy yet."

Just a boy? Wasn't he accepting a man's responsibility? Wasn't he supporting his family? He was so mad he would not speak to his father for a month, even though the war had ended by then.

The flu epidemic of 1918 killed thousands of people all over the world. It reached into the Metzler family as well and put Paul to bed. His youngest brother Ralph went with neighbors to a victory parade to celebrate the Allied victories; but when he came home, the six-year-old also went to bed with the flu. He never recovered.

Paul himself had a sudden relapse and almost died soon after, but God had more plans for his life. During the long hours of convalescence the bored young man picked up the New Testament he had received as a reward for memorization in Sunday School.

"Hey, th-this isn't so b-bad after all."

With mounting excitement, he devoured page after page, figuring out ways to apply it to his life.

Even after he recovered from the flu and returned to work, Paul continued to apply Biblical truths to life around him. He had been put in charge of a crew that tore down machinery used for ammunitions manufacture and replaced it with machinery to make automobiles.

"Take a look at this," the master mechanic called to Paul one day. He waved his hand over the page. "These are the blueprints for the peacetime factory."

They bent over the table for a good look.

"Hey!" Paul exclaimed. "L-Look at all the lines! Someone s-stayed awake nights f-figuring this one out."

"Of course it's detailed. Everything has to be in its own special place so we can keep working smoothly. If they had forgotten anything, everything would probably get mixed up."

"H-Hey," Paul interjected, "that s-sounds like being a Ch-Christian."

"A Christian?!" The master glanced up. "What's that got to do with anything?"

"Well," the young man began slowly, "n-no m-matter how s-small or ins-significant one f-feels, God has a p-place on His b-blueprint for him." He paused a minute. "If we each f-find that place, l-life can go on s-smoothly." He talked faster as his confidence grew. "Of c-course God is a b-better judge of a p-plan for our lives th-than we are, j-just like y-you know better than the m-machines wh-where to put them."

He ended triumphantly. He really must have learned a lot as a kid in Sunday School.

Scree-eech!

Paul jumped.

"Wh-What was that?"

The master mechanic groped for the control switch and suddenly . . . absolute silence.

"Isn't that s-something?" Paul marveled. "Every m-machine has to be s-stopped until the trouble-maker can be f-fixed."

"Yes," his companion snorted, "and time is money. Come on. Let's find the problem."

"But d-don't you see it?" he persisted. "Ch-Christians cause God's work to g-go 'out of commission' b-because we are not doing our work the w-way He wants us to. Th-Then everyth-thing gets bogged down. . . ."

"Come on!" The master mechanic grabbed his arm and pulled him out of the office. "Start over there."

Paul learned to share Bible truths without taking up company time. Working thirty feet in the air on a "sling" one day, he unconsciously whistled a verse of "He Leadeth Me." Then he began to sing.

"Hey," a coworker called, "do you really believe God cares for people? Will He really lead their lives for them?"

"S-Sure," came the confident reply. "God s-says so."

"But what proof is there?"

Proof? That stumped Paul. What could he say to convince this other fellow?

A few days later as the two again worked together, the ropes holding their "sling" slipped. Paul shouted to his partner who scrambled to the top, but Paul was left hanging in midair. He heaved himself up and clung to one of the stronger ropes, but he had to keep away from the hot wires swaying close by. Someone finally brought a ladder, and the two gratefully descended. Paul's partner kept staring back up at the scene of their close call.

"You were right," he told Paul. "God must care what happens to you. No one else could possibly have helped you hold on that long without getting fried."

That confession made the ordeal worthwhile.

Ever since he had quit school, Paul's intense teenage desire for acceptance kept driving him from a life of Bible meditation to a life of worldliness and back again. He remained active in Sunday School and the young people's group, but he also smoked and attended dances and movies. The inner struggle of this double lifestyle fed the dissatisfactions of youth. He had to work when he really wanted to go to school and become a doctor. He could just see himself in a white lab coat with a stethoscope hanging around his neck. While he slaved away, other boys went off to school—boys who did not even care if they went. It was not fair!

Some said that one should trust in God for life's best, while others said that one should go out and take what he wanted from life. Who was right? How could the teenager find out? Would the frustration never end? What good was life like this? Why not just end it all? No one understood, anyway.

The young man finally turned to God.

"L-Lord, I don't even kn-know whether to b-believe in You a-at all anym-more," he cried out. "I-If You'll only d-do s-something f-for me and s-show me that You l-love me and th-that You a-actually exist, I'll d-do anyth-thing in r-return. If Y-You're a G-God of l-love, wh-why d-do I h-have to w-work all the t-time ins-instead of g-going to sch-school? I d-don't want to sp-spend the r-rest of my l-life in f-factories."

The response was not immediate, but God sent the Reverend Bob Moyer to be the evangelist at a revival at church. Hey, this man could preach! He used words, expressions and gestures that could make his audience cry or laugh. Paul was spellbound. He still stuttered, and friends still teased him. He promised himself that someday he would move people by his speech too.

"P-Pastor," the young man ventured, "wh-where did Rev. M-Moyer g-go to sch-school?"

"Why, Paul," came the pleased reply, "are you interested? That's great! He graduated from Moody Bible Institute in Chicago. You'll make a fine preacher, my boy."

Preacher? Nothing could have been farther from his mind, but why

18

disappoint the pastor? Besides, he was too busy trying to figure out how to convince his father to let him go for him to waste time explaining. He went right home to give it a try before he lost his courage.

"F-Father," he plunged in, "you d-didn't l-let me enter the a-army wh-when I wanted to, b-but s-surely now you'll l-let m-me go a m-mere n-ninety m-miles away to Ch-Chicago to sch-school."

After some thought his father agreed. Paul could hardly believe it. It had to be a miracle!

When Paul wrote to inquire, however, he found himself too young to enroll in day classes and too short on funds. What could he do? Advice came from Moody to come anyway and enroll in evening classes and find a job. He was really going away to school! Life suddenly became worth living.

CHAPTER
2

Paul is saved, is specifically trained, and goes to France to learn French as a missionary.

He moved into Osburn Row as soon as he could make the arrangements. The new student drank in every lecture and pored over his studies. His desire to learn could not be quenched, so he begged to be allowed in the day classes.

"OK, Paul, you're in," the Superintendent of Men announced, smiling. "However, I must remind you that since you're still under age, I can't register you as a day student. That means no diploma."

"Th-That's no p-problem," Paul quickly replied. "I c-came here to l-learn. A p-piece of p-paper won't make any d-difference. B-Besides," he continued sheepishly, "I already l-landed a part-time j-job so I can c-come."

The eager student worked so hard that first semester that the faculty gave special permission to accept him as a regular student. What an honor!

In addition to classes, students had practical work assignments each semester. Paul helped with open-air meetings in downtown Chicago. Every week the group drove to a street corner and lowered a platform from the back end of a bus. Some sang, and others played their instruments. At Paul's first street meeting, the leader called on him.

"Come on up and give your testimony for the folks."

What could he say? He knew he had still not trusted Christ as his personal Savior. It was not really necessary—or was it? After a brief "testimony," quickly forgotten, he heaved a sigh of relief to be off the platform. However, he thought about it all the way back to school.

I'm a church member, too, he reminded himself, but these other young people have something I don't. I wonder what it is. How can I find out?

Once again it seemed that God took His time satisfying the boy's spiritual needs. With characteristically perfect timing, however, the Lord sent Lance Latham.

"I've got a great idea, Paul," this fellow student said. "Why don't you bunk in my room? Then we can get up early and play tennis without disturbing anyone else."

"Th-That's a g-great idea!"

They did not waste time getting moved.

"Let's read a chapter of the Word of God before going to bed," Lance suggested that first night.

Paul quickly agreed. They opened the Bible to Romans 8 and read: "There is therefore now no condemnation to them which are in Christ Jesus, who walk not after the flesh, but after the Spirit" (v. 1).

"P-please exp-p-plain this to me," Paul begged.

Lance patiently explained the many verses in Romans 8. When they knelt to pray before finally retiring at two o'clock the next morning, Paul poured out his heart in thanksgiving to the Lord for taking his place at Calvary.*

Years later he recalled that night in a testimony:

"I already knew the facts concerning the life of Jesus; but as we discussed this verse, I realized that when Jesus hung on the cross, He was there in my stead. Because of my own sins I was already condemned, and it wasn't only a matter of the judgment to come after death. For the first time I understood that the wrath of God had been poured out on His Son on the cross, and that anyone who puts total trust in Him is no longer the object of His wrath."

The next day everything had changed. The sun seemed to shine brighter than usual, and the birds seemed to sing more sweetly. Paul began to realize that God had answered the working boy's prayer— He had done something and had shown Himself alive. No, the world had not changed, but Paul Metzler's heart had! Jesus Christ was now his Savior, and the Lord could lead him anywhere He chose.

Just a few days later a missionary spoke in chapel. For the first time Paul heard of people in another country who knew nothing of this joy that he had recently found. Each time a missionary presented the needs of his particular field throughout the semester, this zealous new convert wanted to go there to help.

In the meantime he took advantage of every opportunity to preach in street meetings, at missions or in churches. In addition, he regularly spent Sundays visiting at Cook County Hospital or witnessing in a jail. Quite a change in habit for one who formerly had been severely self-conscious about his speech!

Sickness often interrupted Paul's studies at Moody. Once when he had to go home, he asked to be baptized.

"But Paul," some church leaders objected, "you've already been baptized and accepted into the church."

"I know," he admitted, "but that wasn't a true baptism. I did it only to satisfy the requirements to join the church. I wasn't really saved."

"You weren't?" Pastor M. E. Hawkins asked in surprise. "Well, in that case, of course you can be baptized."

Overjoyed, Paul submitted to the ordinance as soon as he could. That act of obedience fulfilled, he was ready to return to Moody when the time came.

---

*Lance Latham went on from Moody to serve the Lord for many years, helping to start the Awana Club programs. He died January 15, 1985, at the age of ninety.

The young man lived by faith at Moody, learning the power of God to answer prayer. He often saw the Lord work in marvelous ways.

One street meeting at the Sunshine Mission seemed doomed. It was pouring rain when the students started out, but they asked the Lord to make the meeting possible. It was still raining when they took the folding organ and songbooks from the bus and started for their spot. When they arrived, the rain ceased! Not a drop fell as they sang and witnessed. The Lord had prepared receptive hearts, and a number of listeners followed the students into the mission afterward to talk. Many were saved.

During this time Paul sat in classes mornings, worked afternoons and studied into the wee hours in order to be ready for school again the next morning. No wonder illness had often interrupted his studies. Finally his already fragile health broke, and he returned to Mishawaka.

"You simply can't keep up this schedule of working and studying," the doctor told him. "You have got to quit one of them."

What could the boy do? He certainly did not want to give up his studies. As he prayed for help, the Lord made sure that the young men's Sunday School class at First Baptist learned about their teacher's dilemma. They called a special meeting.

"You go back to school," they told him, "and each week we'll send the money for your room and board. That way the doctor will let you go."

Praise the Lord! One member of the class even decided to accompany Paul.

"You were right," Guy McLain confessed to his friend. "As a Christian I do need to give the Lord direction of my life. I don't have enough money, but I believe the Lord wants me to go with you to Moody. I'll just have to trust Him to get me through."*

They found a room outside the Institute. They paid the rent with gifts from the young men's class and managed to live on what they could earn.

By the beginning of 1921, nineteen-year-old Paul decided to return to high school to fill in his faulty educational background. As a result of high performance on a reentry examination, the eighth-grade dropout became a senior and proudly returned the next fall to Moody as a high school graduate.

The spring of 1922 found Paul once again in Mishawaka. At that time the schedule at Moody was operated in "cycles." Having had to

---

*Guy McLain later served many years as a missionary in Brazil.

drop out several times, Paul was now out of cycle, so he found a job while waiting to get back into it. As much as possible he worked in the church and preached in country churches and on the street corners of town.

"Hey, Paul," Pastor Hawkins called from his car as he pulled up to the house. "I got another letter from Rev. Haas."

He walked up and sat beside the boy on the porch steps.

"Remember when I wrote you at Moody about him? Well, more young people are now interested in the work in French Equatorial Africa."

"Oh, yes, I remember. He spoke at Moody, too, but I was home when he was there. I just keep missing him."

"Well, if you remember, he is the founder of a new mission. It's called, um, something like . . . oh, the General Council of Cooperating Baptist Missions of North America."

Paul laughed.

"What a name."

Pastor Hawkins shrugged.

"Just call it GCCBM for short," he suggested with a grin.

"But anyway," he continued more seriously, "Rev. Haas is going all over the United States to arouse interest and support for the mission, especially for his African field. He needs men like you, my boy. What about it?"

Paul thought a minute.

"Well . . . I've often thought about foreign missions. . . . There'd be a lot of work on such a new field, but . . . I guess someone has to do it. Besides, tropical weather'll probably be good for me." He grinned.

Pastor Hawkins slapped his knee.

"Good for you! Now, let's go write your letter."

They let the door slam as they strode inside.

* * *

"Any mail for me today?"

"No. I'm sorry," Mrs. Metzler had to say.

"Just like yesterday," he complained. "And the day before, and the day before that, and the day before that."

He shot his little brother a warning look. Maybe he would receive the response tomorrow. He waited weeks. Finally he sent off another application letter just in case the first one had been lost in the mail. The reply came in a few days.

"The General Councilor of the Mission will be at church Sunday!" the young man exploded, letter in hand. "And he wants to meet me!"

"How soon will you be ready to leave, Paul?" Mr. Carman asked that Sunday.

"Tomorrow, as far as I'm concerned."

Two weeks later, on March 22, 1922, the new missionary boarded the train for New York City. He did not have enough money to get there, much less to reach Africa. The Lord paid for each step of the way as Christians responded to Paul's testimony in Elyria and Columbus, Ohio, and Washington, D.C.

Pastor Haldeman of the First Baptist Church of New York City fellowshipped with Paul when he arrived in New York.

"I don't usually do this," he announced that night at church, "but we have a young missionary here with a heart-stirring testimony. Come on up, Paul, and tell them what you told me this afternoon."

It seemed so long ago that the invitation to give his testimony had terrified the young man. Now he could hardly wait to get started. At the close of the service, the pastor made another announcement.

"I know this is highly irregular, but I'm going to put an offering plate at the door for anyone who would like to help send this young man on his way to Africa. Give as the Lord lays it on your heart."

These Christians, although not prepared for an offering, gave enough to pay Paul's passage. What an answer to prayer!

On the advice of General Councilor Carman, the young missionary went to England before proceeding to France for language study. He stopped by to visit the Rev. and Mrs. C. T. Studd, who had served with William Haas in Africa. The Rev. Studd was now the director of the Heart of Africa Mission. He happened to be away, but his wife had exciting stories to tell her eager guest. Cold weather plagued the trip, however, so the young man was glad to head to balmy France.

During the voyage across the English Channel, Paul met the director of a well-known faith mission.

"An independent Baptist faith mission board?" the director asked. "How is it set up? What is the financial allowance?"

"Oh, I'll get whatever people send in to the Mission for me," Paul replied.

"No allowance? How do you expect to live and pay the expenses of the work?"

"My church and many friends have promised to pray for me, and I expect the Lord to supply my needs."

"You're making a big mistake, my friend. People quickly forget promises. You may starve to death!"

"But I'm not depending only on the people's promises," Paul confidently proclaimed. "I'm depending on God's promise to supply my needs. Besides, I've already seen God work on my behalf."

The director left, shaking his head.

When he arrived at Calais on the northern coast of France, Paul carefully sent a telegram to Miss Mary Bonar telling when he would arrive. She was a missionary studying in Paris. She would know what he should do next. He did not realize that there were a half dozen train stations in Paris, so he did not specify which one. Of course, no one met him. He felt so alone! Now what would he do?

He did manage to get through customs somehow, and then found himself on the sidewalk in front of the station with his two footlockers and suitcase. Now what? He dug in his pocket for the address of the pastor of a Baptist church in Paris and flagged down a taxi.

Paul pointed to his luggage, then to the top of the vehicle. The driver shook his head while Paul nodded. Finally the American shrugged, handed the address to the driver and hoisted up his own luggage.

The newcomer looked in vain for a button to press at Monsieur Arthur Blocher's door. He finally noticed a chain on the wall and gave the handle a jerk. Ah, yes, it was tinkling far inside.

"I might as well pay you now," Paul said as he turned back to the driver. "Hmm." He flipped through some French bills. "Which is big enough for the fare?" He selected one and held it out. "You don't understand my words," Paul said with a smile, "but I'm sure you'll understand this."

Unintelligible sounds burst from the driver, and Paul melted. What in the world could be wrong? The pastor's daughter opened the door just then, and the frustrated driver turned to her. She listened a minute, then took the money back into the house. The driver glared at the dumbfounded foreigner. Shortly, the woman returned and paid up.

"Monsieur Metzler," she explained with a chuckle to her over-whelmed guest, "you gave him one of the biggest bills in French currency. The poor man did not have enough change."

Paul could not help chuckling himself as he followed his benefactor into the living room.

"We have made arrangements for you to stay at the Institut Biblique in Nogent-sur-Marne," Pastor Blocher told his guest. "That is a suburb of Paris. We would like to protect you from irate taxi drivers on your way over," he grinned, "but we just cannot take the time ourselves."

"There is a retired missionary here who will help," Mademoiselle

Blocher added, "but he does not know a word of English." She grinned. "Welcome to France, Monsieur."

First, the two men took the subway. At the end of its route, they transferred to the streetcar. Late afternoon riders had crowded in until only the outside platform on the back had any room left. One by one passengers departed along the way, and soon Paul spied empty seats inside. He made his way up toward the front and sat down. If his companion wanted to remain standing, that was his business.

Before long the lady conductor came back and spoke to the American. Of course he did not understand, so he just smiled at her. She grew more and more animated until she finally gave up in disgust. What could she have wanted?

"Monsieur," came the explanation later, "you purchased a ticket to stand on the platform behind the streetcar. That is the cheapest. The back end is second class, and seats up front sell at first class premiums."

No wonder the poor conductress had been angry. There was so much to learn! If only he knew the language, he sighed. He enrolled in the Alliance Francaise the next day to study French, but it was already several weeks into the course.

"I really need a tutor," he told the director of the Institut Biblique. "Is there another student who could help me?"

* * *

Footsteps on deck on the *S. S. Thysville* interrupted Paul's reminiscing.

"That's all the picture-taking for me," his companion said, laughing as he walked up. "So, are you back with the here and now?"

Paul chuckled. "Guess so."

His friend leaned on the rail, too, and the two men continued the conversation started earlier.

CHAPTER
3

The Lord nurtures Etiennette as she grows up, and gives her an assurance of her salvation while she is studying in England.

While Paul was still sailing for Africa, a special young lady several hundred miles away sat in the study hall of the Institut Biblique of Nogent-sur-Marne in a suburb of Paris. It was study time and she really was trying to study, but her thoughts would not be held down. Instead they were, like Paul's, traveling back over the years, marveling at the way in which the Lord had worked.

Etiennette Emilienne Luc was born by God's grace in Rochefort-sur-Mer on the southwestern coast of France. While she was still young, her parents decided that raising three girls and a boy in town was too hard, so they bought an old house in the little nearby village of Moeze. Etiennette's father worked in an arsenal for the French Navy, and also fished the river and the Atlantic to make a living. Sometimes Etiennette sold the fish for him.

She made friends even though hers was the only Protestant family in the whole village. Many times the priest met her as she came home from school.

"See these pretty pictures?" he asked. "If you come to catechism with your friends, you will get some of these too."

Etiennette ran home to beg her mother to let her go.

"Please! Everyone has them. You want me to learn about God, don't you?"

The Lucs had realized the need for Biblical instruction for the children, but they held to their Protestant beliefs. What could they do? The only solution was to move back to Rochefort when Etiennette was twelve years old.

The Lord had wonderfully arranged for her family to live in a five-room apartment that belonged to the Reformed Church of Rochefort. Her mother became concierge (caretaker) of the apartment building and janitor of the church.

The first year was a hard one for the family. Having been used to the country with plenty of fresh air and room for playing outside, the children found the close life in town was too much for them. One by one they contracted the neighborhood diseases: measles, mumps, chicken pox, whooping cough, croup and typhoid fever.

Etiennette had typhoid the worst. All of her lovely dark, thick tresses had to be shaved off, and she was wrapped in ice sheets to bring down her fever. The doctor even gave up hope. However, he did not know that God had a plan for her future and that to Him death must give way.

A short time after Etiennette had recovered from the typhoid, she fell and broke her leg while jumping rope. Her mother had washed the hallway, sidewalk and courtyard as she did every Saturday afternoon, and they were still slippery.

"Lend a hand!" her father called to a neighbor. "We had better get her to the hospital."

"Oh no, Papa," the poor girl cried. "Not back there. I only just came home."

Pain kept her up all night, though, and the next day she knew she had no choice.

Etiennette had many visitors during her twenty-one days in the hospital. Because they were allowed only a few hours on Sunday and Thursday afternoons, everyone crowded in at once. One gentleman who sat at the girl's bedside waiting his turn was an Englishman working for an English coal company. He had trusted Christ and went to the Lucs' church, often getting involved in youth activities.

As the ladies continued to chat, he glanced around for something to occupy his time. A little notebook lay on a nearby stand, so he picked it up and glanced through it. A diary! No, more of a journal of daily thoughts. He chuckled over several entries, but grew sober at one page. Etiennette had written it on a visiting day.

"It rained today, and nobody came to see me."

Then, at the bottom of the page had been added: "But Jesus was with me all day."

He remembered that this girl had asked especially thoughtful questions in Sunday School. She had even been interested in discussions about the Bible when he visited in her home.

"Lord," Mr. Stamp prayed silently, "I asked You to lead me to young people whom I can help to be used spiritually in France. You know the need here. Is Mademoiselle Luc one You've chosen? Please give me wisdom."

When he left the hospital later, the Englishman approached Etiennette's parents about her future.

"I know she really wants to stay in school and become a teacher, but she is the oldest," Monsieur Luc replied. "We want her to take up a trade that she can use to help the family. That is how we do things in this country. Besides, we cannot afford to keep her in school."

"Sir," Mr. Stamp eagerly offered, "if you let your daughter go on with her schooling, I will be glad to pay for her books."

"That is very generous of you!" the father exclaimed. After thinking a minute, however, he added, "But I cannot see how the sacrifice can be possible."

Several minutes of discussion did finally persuade Monsieur Luc, and planning began.

The coal company decided later to send Mr. Stamp to Germany, so he stopped by the Lucs' to remind them of his promise and to add that he would be back. Soon after he left, the family wrote several times to their friend. Weeks passed, but no answer came. What could have gone wrong? Why did he not write?

For awhile Etiennette's parents did keep her in school, but they could not continue for long without Mr. Stamp's aid. Friends were no help.

"You see," they scoffed, "that Englishman has left and has forgotten all about you."

The Lucs themselves began to believe it as time went on. Finally Monsieur Luc said that Etiennette must learn a trade. Given her choice, she became an apprentice seamstress. She just learned for the first two years, then began earning a salary the third year—all of ten cents a week.

Mr. Stamp reappeared unannounced one day.

"Why didn't you answer my letters?" he asked.

"Your letters? We wrote, but you never answered," Monsieur Luc countered.

A little investigation disclosed that their letters were among thousands being stopped at the frontier between France and Germany because of Germany's warlike tendencies, and never sent on. What a twist of God's providence! Etiennette had become a seamstress because of international unrest!

"OK, Etiennette has certainly learned a useful skill," Mr. Stamp admitted one evening at the Lucs' home. "But I'm awfully disappointed that she had to drop out of school. Now she's three years behind the others. We have to come up with a way to get her education made up as quickly as possible."

They prayed for wisdom before Mr. Stamp went home. A few days later he knocked at the kitchen door.

"We'll send Etiennette to England for a year," he announced. "She can learn English while she's catching up. That way she'll be able to read all the good Christian literature that's available in English but not in French. That'll make her a better Christian as well as a better teacher."

The Lucs agreed when Mademoiselle Flament, Mr. Stamp's fiancée, offered to take the girl with her the next time she went to England. Etiennette hurried down to get her passport.

"How long do you plan to stay, Mademoiselle?"

"Well," she hesitated, "I guess I will return when the war is over."

After all, she thought to herself, I have had a little English in school already, so it should only take a few months to learn it well. Besides,

I have heard that the new weapons being used will quickly end the war. I would just as soon be gone during a war anyway.*

The authorities wrote "for the duration" on her passport, and the fifteen-year-old was off to England. What an exciting trip! However, England itself was not so exciting—no one understood her grade-school English. Worse yet, she could not understand a thing, and no one spoke French.

The poor girl cried herself to sleep the first several nights. Then for two weeks she just gazed at the moon and wondered if her mother was watching it too. She even began planning how to run away, but had to abandon the idea when she realized she could not possibly swim the English Channel.

For the first few months she stayed with Mr. and Mrs. Jones in Houghton-le-Spring, Durham. She taught their young son and daughter French in exchange for her English lessons. They were extremely kind to her and even arranged for her to take organ lessons.

Then she moved to Sunderland to live with the Edwards family, who had a daughter about her age. Etiennette found herself included in the group of girls with whom Maggie associated, spending many wonderful Saturdays hiking far and wide. Not only did her homesickness fade, but before long she felt quite at home in England.

"Etiennette," Maggie suggested one day, "why don't you think about giving French lessons here? Then you'll have your own spending money. You know I give typing lessons to children. You already have experience, too, with the Jones children."

Earn money just to spend? The French girl had never dreamed of such independence! The two friends composed an advertisement for the newspaper:

"Young French girl, newly arrived, will give French lessons at home. Contact Box #18."

Letters poured in from men and women of all ages. The doorbell rang one day, and there stood an army officer in dress uniform with an English-French dictionary.

"Does everyone in England want to learn French?" exclaimed Etiennette when he had gone.

The girls grabbed the paper and found their ad. They stared at each other a minute, then burst into giggles. They had forgotten to specify that they wanted only young children. No wonder the confusion.

Etiennette waded through the mail and finally accepted a dozen children for an hour's lesson twice a week.

---

* World War I

Maggie's father taught a Sunday School class and often served as a lay preacher at the downtown street meeting Sunday nights after church. The whole family always joined in the singing and testimonies. One time, however, Maggie and her mother had gone away Sunday afternoon and did not expect to return until very late. With half his ensemble gone, the lay preacher skipped the singing that night and began to preach right away.

"Now we have a special treat," he announced when he was finished. "A young French girl will give her testimony."

Etiennette stared at him. What would she say? She had not yet learned enough English to make a whole speech. She managed to piece together enough phrases to satisfy everyone and heaved a sigh of relief.

She had been initiated into active service that night and continued to be called on to participate. Each English testimony came easier than the last. It seemed that she had always loved the Lord with all her heart, although the Reformed church back home did not preach conversion. What she knew of Christ, she had learned at an early age from her mother. All this testifying and singing praises to God brought a warm assurance that she had been converted by the grace of God. What a joy! She wrote all her friends in France to tell them.

At long last it was time to return to France and reenter school. Etiennette stopped by the passport office to be sure all was well.

"But Mademoiselle," the officer protested, "you cannot return until the war is over. See, your passport says, 'for the duration.' "

"But when will the war be over?" she naively asked.

The officer burst into laughter. Surely she was not serious! The poor girl's disheartened look finally sobered the man, however, and he advised her to write to the French authorities for permission to reenter because of schooling.

CHAPTER
4

The Lord protects Etiennette in London during World War I, leads her home and continues her training. She meets Paul and they become engaged.

By this time Etiennette had already left the Edwards' and was staying in London with friends of Mr. Stamp. She spent eleven days there, waiting for the answer to her request. The zeppelins (German dirigibles) floated over London nearly every night. (Sunderland had already had many alerts.) No lights were allowed on the streets after dark. Anyone who went walking late had to wear a large fluorescent button so that he or she could be seen, and had to call "Look out! Look out!" as an added precaution.

Knock! Knock! Knock!

A bobby (policeman) stood at the door, frowning. Etiennette's eyes widened, and she swallowed hard. What could have happened? She stepped back as he marched in.

"The blinds, mates, the blinds!" he scolded, waving toward the windows. "Do you want the bloody zeppelin to spot you?"

The family scrambled to pull the shades. They would be safe now. They knew the light could not leak out around the blinds because they had pasted dark blue paper along the edges of the windows.

The zeppelins usually came about dusk. The alarm bellowed, and bobbies bicycled through the streets shouting "Clear out! Clear out!" Normal bustling peaked as everyone dashed home or ducked into an underground shelter. The terror would come in less than an hour.

Etiennette and her hosts dropped what they were doing and ran through the house locking the doors and closing the shutters. Then they hurried to the cellar. They crawled under a large table and sandwiched themselves between pillows.

The whole world held its breath. When would the onslaught come? Waiting . . . waiting . . . waiting. . . . This dreadful waiting!

Gradually they heard it. Faraway bombs screamed and then exploded one after another. The guns from the Tower of London drummed back at them. Shells whistled as they fell back to the ground. Then silence. Was it over? As if in answer, the screaming and crashing and whistling began again, only a little closer. Then silence again. When would it start back up?

Crash!

Silence.

Crash!

The percussions of war crept nearer each time. Minutes seemed like hours. Etiennette squeezed her pillow tighter. Would the next bomb fall on them?

Wheeee!

Crash!

Kerblam!

The locked doors and windows at Etiennette's hideout burst open. Smoke billowed in, and she buried her head deeper into the pillows and cried for her mother. When the next explosion sounded a little farther off, choking neighbors ran to their doors to investigate.

Dogs howled. Women chattered hysterically. Men wandered in the streets in their bathrobes and nightcaps. Soon the streets again overflowed with people. Bobbies begged them to go back home because the zeppelins might return, but no one listened.

The bomb had left a large crater in the middle of the house across the street. Bobbies had roped it off and were forming a circle around it to try to keep the people away, but a curious crowd stretched to peer down inside. Praise the Lord, the family who lived there had joined in the evacuation of London the day before!

Part of the house lay in a heap. Inside, part of a cupboard seemed to be suspended in midair, with pots and pans still hanging. One woman fainted and was carried to her house. Etiennette's friends decided that they would take their guest to the official underground shelter for added safety.

The stranded French girl knew she would never forget the underground shelter. The bobbies did their best to create a cheerful atmosphere in the shelter, but it was always in vain. Mostly women and children crowded in, and the children, sensing danger, usually cried and clung to their mothers' skirts. Anxious bobbies often asked the oldest of the children to sing or recite, but none ever had the courage.

One night a frustrated bobby decided he would have to be the one to entertain the crowd. He stood on a chair in the middle of the room and began singing. The more he sang, the more the children cried. Finally he gave up in despair.

Hush! What was that? Shouting in the street above? What was going on? Mothers stifled their children's sobs. Some stood up. Others edged toward the door. Outside, feet pounded up to the door.

"It's hit!"

The shelter was now deathly still.

"The zeppelin! It's burning."

"Hurrah!"

Tension exploded.

"Hurrah!"

No more fear. Everyone swept toward the door.

"Stay inside, mates," came sharply over the noise. "We cannot be sure whether it really was a German zeppelin or actually one of our planes."

An English plane? That hushed the crowd. The tension built again.

"It is!" panted the messenger. "A zeppelin!"

"Hurrah!"

Bobbies creaked open the door. Everyone shot out and raced the few miles out of town where the zeppelin was slowly coming down in flames. The crowd hushed as the inferno came closer to earth. They gave silence to the two men inside who also burned to charcoal.

* * *

What a relief when Etiennette was at last allowed to leave London! She traveled to Southampton where a boat took her to Saint-Malo, France. It felt so good to once again stand on French soil! Oh, there might be a little adjustment after being so immersed in English, but this was home.

Just to be sure, the teenager practiced asking the way to the train station over and over. Then she walked up to a lady to try it out.

"Excuse me, madame, could you tell me how to get to the train station?"

English! How could that have happened? She tried several times, but it was always the same. The woman just smiled at her and shrugged. A year ago the student had had trouble communicating in a foreign land, but now she was having trouble communicating in her mother tongue. She must practice harder.

By this time Mr. Stamp had married and had started a mission in Saint-Brieuc in northern France. Etiennette went directly there to resume her studies.

The first few days in class were awful. She had forgotten how to spell in French, and her tongue always pronounced the letters in English. The other girls exploded into laughter, nearly bringing tears to the poor newcomer's eyes. What would she do? A friend in the next seat came to the rescue by pronouncing the letters one by one in French for Etiennette to repeat. Of course she quickly remembered.

After two years Etiennette returned to Rochefort and spent about a year finishing her basic course. She could not take her more advanced teacher's training at home, however, so she had to go to a boarding school for two more years.

Most of her life Etiennette had wanted to be a missionary. As a little girl she often lined up her dolls to make a congregation.

"Now, you girls know how naughty you are sometimes," she wagged her finger at them. "You need to ask Jesus to clean all that sin out of your heart. Then you can be His little girl too. Then He can make you good little girls and make Mama and me proud of you."

"Who are you talking to, Etiennette?" her amused mother asked.

"Oh, I am preaching to African children, Mama. They wriggle, but they listen."

However, during her two years at the boarding school the girl did not have her mother's godly influence. Instead, she listened more and more to a teacher who seemed to know more than anyone else in the world.

"You were in London during the war," the teacher prompted. "Did you see God at work in the bombs or fires or deaths? Of course not. If there were a God, He should have been able to do something about it. No God, no Bible. You have to face up to the real world, Etiennette."

The graduate returned home and announced, "I have changed my mind about becoming a missionary. It would be a waste of time. I will write to Mr. Stamp right away."

What could her parents do? As if in answer, the girl received a letter from Mr. Stamp a few days later.

"A round-trip ticket to Switzerland," she gasped, "for a two-week holiday!"

She lowered the letter to her lap. Switzerland! Snowcapped mountains! Picturesque chalets!

"A graduation gift?" her mother cut into her dreams.

"Yes," the girl blinked. "I do not think it will hurt anything to wait until after the trip to tell him the change of plans." She glanced at her mother. "Do you?"

Mr. Stamp had made reservations for his young friend at a Bible conference grounds directed by Dr. Ruben Saillens, a prominent French Baptist preacher and a great man of God. It seemed to Etiennette that every appeal to young people was directed at her. This was not at all what she had had in mind for a vacation in Switzerland.

The third day she could no longer hold back but dedicated her life to the Lord for service wherever He would have her go. She knew the Lord she had begun to doubt had sent her here for this purpose.

"When I get back to Paris this September," Dr. Saillens announced later, "I will open a Bible school, the Lord willing. This is the first one in France to train French men and women who desire to serve the Lord. Please see me for more information."

Etiennette enrolled immediately—the first girl to do so. Instead of going back home after her holiday, she went straight to Paris and wrote to her mother, asking her to please send her trunk to the Institut Biblique of Nogent-sur-Marne. Then she wrote a much different letter than originally planned to Mr. Stamp to tell him the good news.

She greatly enjoyed studying God's Word, discovering wonderful new truths nearly every day. She knew the needs in France and thought of home mission service. Then in class she heard about other lands where there was no gospel witness at all. Which country should she choose? Africa? As a child she had dreamed of it. She would have to pray about it.

Now how would she pay for her schooling? With her experience from England in mind, Mademoiselle Luc arranged to teach French to students from the Alliance Francaise. She set up classes with Norwegian, Swedish, English and American missionaries, and then was asked to give private lessons to a young man who had arrived late for the beginning of his course.

"Just remember, Mademoiselle," she was instructed at the Institut Biblique, "you must meet with this young man in a public place—say, the library or school office. We do not want to offend the Parisians. You know how they feel about boys and girls doing everything separately."

Etiennette made the necessary arrangements with her pupil, Paul Metzler, but often he did not show up for the lessons anyway.

"But Mademoiselle," Paul sheepishly explained, "there are so many things to see in Paris! I just couldn't tear myself away from the Louvre today. As it was, I didn't get to examine all the paintings. Tomorrow I promise I'll hurry my friends along—we go to see the Eiffel Tower!—so that I won't miss another lesson."

Etiennette pursed her lips, then spun around and marched off. He was just plain irresponsible, she decided. He spent nine months at the Institut, and she watched him carefully develop an understanding of the French customs and way of thinking. She also noticed that he formed a lifetime of friendships with French Christians. Maybe he was not so irresponsible after all.

In the summer of 1922, Etiennette returned to French Switzerland to work in the bookstore maintained by Dr. Saillens' Bible conference. What an opportunity to serve the Lord by helping the work that had so touched her own life! One day not long after she started her duties she saw—no, it had to be imagination. Her surprise shone back from the face of Paul Metzler!

"Do you come every summer?" he managed to ask.

"No," she answered when she found her voice. "How is it that you are here?"

"Oh, the directors at the Bible institute suggested I come here to rest. It is beautiful here. Lake Geneva just sparkles."

The girl nodded. There was a peace here in the mountains.

Paul laughed.

"Rest? I'm too busy making friends among the Swiss brethren! The

Lord also gives me opportunities to witness and to preach the gospel. I'm having a great time 'resting.' "

Along with his other activities, Paul managed to squeeze in visits to the bookstore. By the time he had to leave Switzerland, he had become a regular customer.

Mademoiselle Luc resumed her tutoring upon their return to Paris, but her relationship with her private student had changed. To sharpen language skills, she had him read in French the life story of missionary Hudson Taylor. Sometimes the chapters ended with discussions that became more and more personal as the days passed.

"I think your private lessons should stop," the dean of women told Paul one day toward the end of his term of study. "You can tell Mademoiselle on Saturday."

"Stop? Why?"

After some discussion Paul reluctantly agreed. On Saturday the dean approached Etiennette.

"Come for a walk with me to the park of Vincennes," she invited.

Especially fond of Mademoiselle Saillens, Etiennette jumped at the chance for her company. As they started out, the dean revealed the real reason for going to the park.

"Monsieur Metzler is waiting to talk to you," she said. "I think you two need to have a long, private discussion."

"What?" Etiennette stopped short. "A long, private discussion? Whatever for?" She paused a moment and frowned, then added, "I do not believe I can go for a walk with you today after all."

She turned to go back, but the dean called to her.

"You two need to talk, and I think the sooner the better," the older woman said firmly. "You do not see it now, but I do. Come along."

Etiennette hesitated, but she knew she could trust her companion's advice. She fell into step again.

"Now remember, you two must come back separately," Mademoiselle Saillens addressed them in the park. She took a step to go, then added with a smile, "and do get this matter settled."

The young people went for a walk to collect their thoughts. Then they sat down on a park bench. Paul took a deep breath.

"God called me into missions and has led me so far," he plunged in. "There isn't anything positively certain about the future, I'm afraid. I don't know exactly where I'm going to work except that it will be in French Equatorial Africa. We'll have to trust God to supply our needs since the mission that I'm with doesn't pay a salary."

He squirmed on his seat as Etiennette stared at him. What could he be trying to say? What did he mean by "we"?

Paul took another deep breath and let it out slowly. Suddenly he relaxed and even smiled.

"I certainly would like you to go along as my wife," he urged, watching her eyes for her response, "but I felt that you should know the circumstances before committing yourself."

Commitment.

Marriage.

"Ooh! La, la!"

Etiennette took a few deep breaths of her own, and then felt the joy of love bubbling up inside her. Although from across the ocean, this man understood her people and loved her country—and her. From their other discussions she knew she could trust herself to his care. Yes, this had to be of the Lord.

The excited couple barely managed to contain themselves through the last weeks of their course. Dr. Saillens had stipulated that their engagement not be announced in Paris until after Paul's departure, so they painstakingly complied. Would it ever end?

The Lord enabled Paul to visit the Luc family for a few days before he had to leave France. The young couple could talk about their relationship there. What a relief! All too soon Etiennette and her mother had to take Paul to a nearby town to board his ship. They stood on the dock waving as he set off for his first trip to Africa.

Etiennette proudly wore her engagement ring back to school. By now the other girls knew the secret and could hardly wait for the details. They surrounded her in the library the first night back and bombarded her with questions. Long-suppressed answers poured out.

"Remember the time even before you met Paul when we were all talking about things we wanted to do?" one girl interjected. "Etiennette, you said that one of your greatest desires is to visit the United States someday. Remember?"

Etiennette nodded and smiled.

"You thought that it would never be possible, but now you are sure to see it one day after all. You will have your own private tour guide too."

The girls giggled, many staring starry-eyed at their privileged friend.

Suddenly Dr. Saillens walked in. What a sobering influence! He glanced sternly around the room, then rested his eyes on Etiennette.

"I would like to comment on the great event that has taken place in this student's life," he said. "I condone it, but strongly advise the rest of you to complete your studies at the Institut before thinking of matrimony. That is the best way."

47

The girls solemnly promised to think seriously about it. Etiennette promised to put her mind to her studies. She still had a year—it seemed more like forever—before she could join her beloved.

"Good," Dr. Saillens said with a nod. "Now this is the evening study hour. Please use it correctly."

* * *

Suddenly Etiennette realized that she was not doing very well at keeping her promise. Her thoughts had been running away with her again. Dutifully she bent her head and started reading the lesson in front of her once more.

CHAPTER
5

**Paul goes to Africa as a missionary
and adjusts before sending
for his fiancée.**

When he sailed from the port of La Pallice, France, Paul Metzler waved back to his fiancée and her mother until he could no longer see them. So much had happened this past year. Come to think of it, a lot had happened over a whole lifetime to get to this point.

The first evening out of port, all the missionaries on board gathered for fellowship around the supper table. Gust Pearson had been at Moody with Paul. Miss Mary Bonar was the schoolteacher whom Paul had written to meet him in Paris when he first arrived. Both had joined Paul's mission. Allen Bennett had studied French at the Alliance Francaise with Paul. He and Dr. Florence Gribble, the only experienced one among them, served with the Brethren Mission.

"Hey, look at this!" one exclaimed when he opened the menu. "Can anyone read this?"

The others reached for menus too. One frowned, one scratched his head, and one sighed.

"It's Flemish," chuckled Dr. Gribble.

What would they do? How could they find out what was on the menu? Then the three young men hit on a plan—they would start at the top and eat down. What a meal!

That first night the ship rolled and pitched in a storm in the Bay of Biscay. Paul breakfasted alone the next morning. At lunch no more than a half dozen people from the entire passenger list of almost three hundred were in the dining room.

Gust Pearson suffered the most from seasickness. He had grave doubts about whether he would ever live to see Africa. Before long he lost interest in seeing Africa at all, and by the third day of the storm he began to fear that he might not die after all. At least death would end the agony.

Just a few days after the storm ended, the ship ran into dense fog that lasted for several days.

Mm Baa! Mm Baa! bellowed the foghorn.

Mm Baa! Mm Baa! All day and all night it blasted its warning.

Mm Baa! Mm Baa! Mm Baa!

Despite the weather, passengers crowded the dance floor on deck each afternoon or sat at the bar. Some organized card games. One day the bow of a freighter crept out of the fog and headed directly for their ship.

"Look out!"

A lady screamed. Frightened passengers dropped to their knees to pray. The captain saw it coming soon enough to turn the *Thysville* so that she bore the force of the oncoming ship broadside.

Thump! Crunch!

The shock knocked several sprawling but caused little damage. The relieved passengers got up from their knees and picked up their cards, repoured their drinks and tuned up the band again.

Paul shook his head. Lost souls expect God's help when disaster strikes but feel no further obligation to Him, he mused. Sadly, he joined the other missionaries in one of the cabins to thank God for His protection.

One morning at breakfast each missionary found a small white pill beside his or her plate.

"That's from me," Dr. Gribble confessed with a smile. "You might as well get used to them because every day you're in Africa, you must take at least one of these pills to protect yourselves from malaria."

The newcomers picked up the little tablets to examine them closer while Dr. Gribble explained further.

"Anopheles mosquitoes flourish in Africa's interior. When they bite you, they inject a blood-thinning fluid that carries the malaria germ. Unless something is in the blood to kill the germ, you'll contract malaria and maybe even develop deadly Blackwater fever. Neither of these is any fun at all," Dr. Gribble grinned. "Now, bottoms up."

Obediently, the newcomers popped the pills into their mouths and reached for a glass of water. What a mistake! This had to be the most bitter medicine any had ever taken. It took most of the day to get the awful taste out of their mouths, and from then on each tried one trick after another to swallow that quinine pill.

Paul spent his time learning as much about this new country as he could from Dr. Gribble. He also took time to write the Mission about how God had led him to Etiennette and how helpful she would be in his ministry. Sometimes, however, the days dragged by, and it seemed that the whole world was painted blue.

Then the shores of Africa came into view. Spirits soared!

"Hey, look at the turtles!"

Passengers flocked on deck to see the giant turtles peering from beneath half-closed eyelids as they basked in the sun.

"Oh," someone gasped, "over there!"

Porpoises leaped from the water like acrobats, chattering their welcome.

"Well," Paul chuckled, "at least the animals are glad to see us."

The missionaries went ashore at Matadi in Belgian Congo (now Zaire).

"Don't forget to buy your train tickets," Dr. Gribble urged a little later. "The rapids in the lower part of the Congo River are not navigable. Hope they will be someday. This is a narrow gauge railroad and has a woodburning locomotive, so it takes two days just to go our 250 miles."

Two days to soak in a new and exciting world? Sounded like fun to the young people.

The first day they chugged slowly uphill. The crew apparently was not in much of a hurry to reach their destination. They even took their time picking out fresh produce at each of the numerous stations along the way. The newcomers decided to try some, too, and discovered that a ripe banana was quite refreshing on hot days such as these.

The missionaries understood the crew's desire to stop for refreshment, but why keep all the windows in the small coaches closed? Why not let in some air? At first they quietly wiped the perspiration from their foreheads, but finally took it upon themselves to open the windows. Ah! The breeze felt so good!

Then the train started to climb the next hill, and that same breeze blew sparks from the chimney of the locomotive through the window and onto Paul's shirt.

"Yeowch!"

He jumped up, pulling his shirt away from him and swatting where it still smoked. The others scrambled to close the windows.

"Just look at that!" exclaimed Mary Bonar, pointing at Paul. "It burned a hole through his shirt."

Quickly the young missionaries decided they would rather smother with the windows up than burn with them down.

Late that evening they at last arrived at the town of Thysville, only to learn that they should have telegraphed ahead for room reservations. Not having done so, the men had to sleep on the veranda of the rest house while the ladies stayed inside. To top it all off, a dog woke the men up while trying to carry off a pair of their shoes.

The next day's trip to Leopoldville (now Kinshasa) was mostly downhill. The Americans decided they preferred the uphill trip despite the inconvenience of sometimes having to back up, get up more steam and make a second try at a hill. As the train shot downhill, the passengers clung to their seats.

"Aren't there any brakes on this thing?" one squeaked out.

At the foot of nearly every hill was a sharp curve with a nearby stream into which they constantly expected to roll. Instinctively, everyone leaned in the opposite direction. The missionaries certainly praised God for guardian angels during that trip!

From Leopoldville they had to cross Stanley Pool, which is formed by the backwaters of Stanley Falls on the Congo River. At Brazzaville (then the capital of French Equatorial Africa) they could catch a river steamer up the Congo to Bangui, the capital of Oubangui Chari Province (now the Central African Republic).

At Brazzaville, however, the missionaries learned that the river steamer had left two days before and would probably return in about three weeks. Three weeks? Now what could they do? They held an emergency prayer meeting, then looked around.

"Hey, over there!"

A small river steamer bobbed near the bank. They eagerly sought out its captain.

"Why, yes," he said, "I'm leaving for Bangui in two days. Of course I'd be happy to have five paying passengers. So happy, in fact, that I'll take your baggage free of charge."

He ran the back of his wrist across his eyes, and then dabbed at his forehead with a stained handkerchief.

"One thing you must know before you decide to sail with me. Instead of making the trip in two weeks like the bigger steamer, it'll take us around twenty days. Also, I don't have cabins. You'll have to furnish your own beds and sleep on the covered deck."

The travelers agreed to the terms and created private quarters for the ladies by stretching a canvas between the front and the back end of the deck. The first few days held magic as the new missionaries watched for birds and monkeys in shoreline trees and for people in the villages or in the many canoes on the river. Several times each day the steamer had to stop to buy or cut firewood for the engine, and each night they tied up at a village or a sandbar since they were not equipped to travel at night. By the end of the first week, however, all this had become rather monotonous.

The sleeping quarters proved quite comfortable until the steamer left the region that was having its dry season and sailed into the rainy season. The adventurers discovered that the roof leaked, especially in the front where sparks from the chimney had burned holes. Many nights the men slept underneath their camp cots instead of on them.

Allen Bennett had a favorite cake of sweet-smelling toilet soap, and had put it in his shoe to preserve it. During one night his shoe was pushed out from under the bed.

Drip! Drip! Drip!

By the next morning the soap had completely dissolved. Allen was heartsick! Now, how should a new missionary deal with minor tragedies?

"Ladeez and gentlemen!" he announced that afternoon. "As a token of my sincere friendship, this previously hoarded soap—my

54

very favorite soap, you know—is now available to one and all."

His audience laughed as he held out a handful of suds.

"Step right up and claim your bubble."

One could almost forget how muggy it was if there were a good enough laugh.

Nineteen days after their departure from Brazzaville and two days before arrival at Bangui, the missionaries saw in the distance a tall, bearded white man in a dugout canoe. One of his companions signaled to the steamer to slow down so the canoe could draw alongside. The tall man climbed aboard and introduced himself as the Rev. William Haas, the founder of the Mid-African Mission. What a welcome diversion.

At Bangui, Allen and Dr. Gribble met Mr. Gribble and left for their mission near the government post of Bozoum. The Rev. Haas arranged for two dugout canoes with crews to take his party of four on up the Oubangui River, a branch of the Congo.

Immediately after leaving Bangui, the Oubangui River breaks into the swift and dangerous Elephant Rapids. The newcomers gripped the sides of their canoes—except one. Paul might as well have been on a duck pond in a rowboat for all the attention he paid the rapids. He sat absorbed in one of the many letters he had received in Bangui— his first letter from his fiancée.

In order to proceed upstream, the canoes had to be poled, and the young men took their turns. They leaned and pushed and grunted and strained against the current, but it often seemed as if they were not advancing at all.

Brother Haas made the time go faster by sharing details of the work and his dreams for it.

"I want to establish a national church in French Equatorial Africa," he said. "It'll have its own national pastor someday."

His eyes sparkled.

"I want to start a work in the territory of Chad too. That's north of the Oubangui Chari district and just south of the Sahara Desert."

He clenched his fist.

"Just as soon as possible. That area isn't yet open to civilians, but the Lord willing, when it does open," he slammed his fist into his other palm, "we'll be ready."

Paul's ears perked up. A completely untouched area. No gospel witness at all.

He even met some Chadians the Sunday after his party arrived at Fort Sibut. The little chapel was packed with people that morning, and they seemed to drink in the words of the Rev. Haas's message. On the front row of logs sat eight or ten men who listened even more attentively than all the rest. They gathered around the Rev. Haas after the service.

"Who are these men?" Paul asked later. "I know they aren't from around here because they're so tall—over six feet, I'd say—and they have those welts on their faces. What did they talk about?"

"Oh, they're from the Sara tribe in the Chad district, and they wanted to know when someone was going to come to their country and tell their people the message I preached this morning."

Paul returned to his hut deep in thought, knelt beside his camp cot and pledged himself to go to the Sara people with the gospel as soon as the Lord would make it possible.

In the meantime he settled down at Fort Sibut to study the language with the Rev. and Mrs. Ferd Rosenau, lending a hand as was needed. The Rosenaus had been on the station only two years themselves and still had much to do.

One hot, sunny day Paul helped Ferd lay stones to make a foundation for a permanent house. Despite the 120-degree heat, the younger missionary began to have chills. He ignored them until his teeth began to chatter and Ferd sent him in to bed.

Paul continued to shiver beneath several woolen blankets. What in the world could be wrong with him? Mrs. Rosenau came in with a big pot of hot tea.

"You have malaria," she insisted at his protest, "and this is the only cure." She poured him a cup. "Now drink this, and I'll give you more later."

Paul could not remember having forgotten to take the little white pill each morning. Why had it not prevented this discomfort? Obviously the medicine was not infallible.

After awhile the woolen blankets and hot tea began to take effect. As the new missionary lay with perspiration soaking his sheets, he could not help but think back to a remark he had heard and later would often hear after meetings in the States: "It must be wonderfully romantic to go into such a primitive country as Africa."

Some romance!

When Paul finally recovered, he heard that Allen Bennett, a companion on the trip to Africa, had died. The Lord had seen fit to take Allen home even before he had reached his mission station, but God had preserved Paul's own life. Sometimes Paul felt heavy with sorrow that a friend could not fulfill his dream to serve the Lord longer, and sometimes he was lifted up with joy for that friend who was now in Heaven with his Lord. The young missionary plunged into the work the Lord had apparently left him on earth to do.

The Rev. Haas and Rev. Rosenau decided that Paul should go to Fort Crampel after he had been in Sibut several months. Crampel was farther north, closer to the Chad district and to the Sara tribe. There Paul worked with the Rev. and Mrs. Young among the Mandjia people, and there he had his first experience in village work. With two or three men carrying his bedding and chop-box, he would make bicycle trips into the bush for a week or two at a time.

On the first trip, wanting to reach a village before dark, the eager missionary peddled ahead of his carriers and found himself in the middle of the plains when night fell. The path divided into several branches, none of which looked familiar.

Roarr!

Other lions joined the chorus from different corners of the darkness.

Hyena cries added the staccato.

Not knowing which way to go, Paul sat down on the side of the road. His eyes darted from side to side but could not penetrate the inkiness.

"What now, Lord?"

Within a few minutes a voice asked, "Mo yeke sala gne?" ("What are you doing?")

The owner of the voice emerged from the blackness, and Paul followed him to safety. What a wonderful answer to prayer!

During this same trip the new missionary hunted and killed an antelope, a reed buck that weighed about 120 pounds. He told the cook to prepare him a few of the choice morsels and then share the rest of the meat with the men. Hardly any of the meat remained the next morning.

"What in the world happened to all that meat?" he asked the cook.

"Remember, Monsieur," the cook responded, "you said we could have the rest of the meat."

Then Paul noticed the men's distended stomachs. Oh, how they must ache! They did not let this stop them, however. That day they walked twenty-four miles to the next village. Paul knew he still had a lot to learn about customs here.

On another bush trip, he visited the post of Batangafou, where a tribe closely related to the Saras lived. They received him well, expressing much interest in the gospel. Several men trusted Christ and later came to Fort Crampel to work and gain a deeper knowledge of the Scriptures.

At their insistence Paul returned to their village in the latter part of

1923 and found a suitable place to set up a mission station. He could work there while waiting for the Chad to open. These plans were disrupted, however, when a telegram announced the imminent arrival of new missionaries at Bangui. Mademoiselle Etiennette Luc was a member of this party, so Paul dashed back to offer his assistance.

CHAPTER
6

**Etiennette follows,
and the two are married.**

A llen Bennett's death was announced to the shocked Institut Biblique student body soon after it happened. Etiennette remembered him as one of her French class pupils, who was always cheerful. Every day heavyhearted classmates pleaded with God to call someone to replace him, and many even dedicated their own lives as his replacements. Allen's death, then, brought much glory to God as many more missionaries volunteered for His service. What a wonderful epitaph!

A few months later the Rev. Haas made it a point to stop in France to visit the Institut. Etiennette's parents met his ship at La Pallice, the port from which Paul had left.

"Yes, young people, we need preachers in the French colonies," he urged at the Institut. "Lots of them. 'And how shall they hear without a preacher?' But," he leaned over the pulpit to study one face after another as he talked, "we need teachers as well."

He paused to push up from the pulpit, never breaking his eye contact.

"The people need to learn how to read the Bible for themselves. We have to train men to take leadership roles. Help me develop a system of education equal to this one you enjoy," he waved a hand toward his spellbound audience. "If France can extend her political boundaries, why shouldn't we expand the boundaries of the Kingdom of God?"

He took a special interest in Etiennette, both for Paul's sake and because she had been trained as a teacher.

"I believe you're the answer to my prayer to begin a school in Africa," he told her. "In fact, can you be ready to go in seven months? I'm going to America next to share the burden and to take all who respond to the field."

Seven months? She would have liked to go to the field right now. Her shining eyes belied the calmness in her voice.

"Oh, yes sir."

The day finally arrived in November 1923 when Etiennette could go to Bordeaux to join the Mid-Africa Mission party. What sweet fellowship she enjoyed with the Rev. Haas, Mr. and Mrs. Camp, Miss Margaret Nicholl, Miss Marie Gantz, Mr. Walter Gantz and Mrs. Laura Bayne.

Often Etiennette would sit on deck humming a tune while watching the sun set into the ocean. The Rev. Haas would join her and play along on his harmonica. Etiennette would then sing the words, and her accompanist would sometimes break into harmony with his rich tenor voice. What wonderful times Christians could have!

"Rev. Haas," Etiennette ventured once, "do you have a picture of your wife that I may see?"

Her heart overflowed with thoughts of marriage. He smiled, his deep blue eyes full of understanding.

"I'd show you a picture if I could," he replied kindly, "but it's engraved on my heart. That way I always have it available when I have to leave my wife behind while I travel."

A smile grew on the girl's face. That is love, she decided.

Like their predecessors, this group left the ocean liner at the coast of Africa and boarded a boat on the Congo River. Would it always be this muggy?

An apple appeared under each pillow the first night out. Who would have placed it there, and why? The grin on William Haas's face gave him away.

"We can't get apples in Africa," he explained, "so I bought two cases of them before leaving the ocean liner. I had planned to distribute them among the missionaries already on the field, but now I'm not so sure these beauties will keep that long in this heat."

He wiped the perspiration from his forehead.

"They'll all go to waste if they don't go to our waist."

He patted his stomach and chuckled.

Haas led devotions every morning in the dining room, and gave Sango lessons to his little group every evening after they gathered up on deck. The scorching afternoons were left open.

The riverboat often stopped at towns and villages along the way. Everyone in the towns came to see the boat and then talked about it for weeks. Not only did the riverboat mean a break in daily monotony, it also meant mail, food from France and fruit. Sometimes the captain extended to a few of the area's French administrators the rich honor of coming on board for a meal.

"Listen up, mates, we are coming to the end of my line," the captain announced one day. "Get your things together tonight, because tomorrow you'll have to transfer to a smaller boat. The river gets too shallow for my tub."

As they neared Bangui the next day, the people on shore edged closer to the water, and the passengers leaned farther out, each trying to recognize the folks coming toward them. Where was Paul? William Haas pulled out his binoculars.

"There he is!"

Etiennette's eyes eagerly followed the outstretched finger. There he was! Etiennette could hardly sit still. Paul seemed extra lanky next to the African nationals he had brought with him to carry the baggage.

How proud she was of him!

"Come on, young lady," Mr. Haas interrupted her thoughts with a smile. He led the way to the captain's cabin.

"Wait here."

The gentleness in his eyes quieted her questions and calmed her impatience.

One of the crew tied the boat to a metal post, and then—*kerplunk!* A plank fell across the gap between the boat and land, and Paul leaped across before it had even been declared safe for passage. He strode along the deck looking for one special face. Mr. Haas took his arm and steered him in the right direction.

The others went ahead and walked the plank to shore. Before too long the glowing couple joined them. Ah! It felt so good to leave the boat and feel solid ground beneath one's feet again. Emotions soared as the new missionaries realized that they had reached French Equatorial Africa. This was their mission field and home for many years, should the Lord tarry.

Was the sun always so intense? What would the new way of life be like? What would the people be like?

Curious, Etiennette stared at the row of Africans who stood stiffly at attention near the shore. When Paul gave a shrill whistle they bounded to the boat, falling all over each other trying to grab the missionaries' baggage. Each one hoisted his load onto his head and solemnly joined his comrades marching away down the road. What a strange scene.

"OK, come on." Haas gestured, and the others fell in step. "First, we'll have to find a place to sleep."

After much searching Paul rented a huge storehouse and set up a folding table in the middle for meals. He then proceeded to buy a metal plate, cup and set of silverware for each member of the party. The men put up their cots and mosquito nets at one end of the building while the ladies made the other end as comfortable as possible. A large piece of canvas stretched across the middle finished the preparations. For several days they remained in Bangui, buying supplies and going through the usual red tape one must face when arriving in a foreign country.

"This prolonged stay suits me just fine," Haas told Paul and Etiennette. "Before my last furlough I became friends with one of the high officials here. I told him I expected to return with a school-teacher."

He winked at Etiennette.

"I want to introduce you to each other first thing. It's always wise

63

here in Africa to work through an official or chief or whoever is in charge. Think I'll pay Monsieur Isembert another visit."

That afternoon Mr. Haas again sought out his two young friends. He could hardly contain his excitement.

"We've been invited for dinner tonight! Now we can lay the groundwork for a school!"

Monsieur Isambert greeted his guests warmly. When they sat down to eat, he pulled out the chair to his right for Etiennette.

"Now, Mademoiselle," he warned energetically, "too many requests for permission from the governor are dry and void of personality. The governor appreciates a personal tone to the letter."

He paused to chew another bite thoughtfully before continuing.

"Mention some of your own reasons for wanting to open a school and add something about your attraction to the little children. So far they have never had a chance to learn to read and write, you know."

Etiennette thanked him for his suggestions, and then followed them when she sat down to write the letter. Surely the governor wanted her to educate his people.

Finally the missionaries began their journey to Fort Sibut. The men had made a "push-push" for each person by fastening a seat between two motorcycle wheels. Handlebars in the front and back allowed one man to pull and one to push.

The newcomers eagerly soaked in each strange new sight, sound or smell they encountered. After traveling their twenty miles for the day, they would stop at a government rest house where Paul and Haas would rustle up a satisfying, if not somewhat unusual, meal. Every night each one had his or her camp cot and mosquito net to put up before collapsing into it, and every morning after breakfast all the camping equipment had to be repacked and each porter's load rearranged. What a job!

As soon as they arrived at Fort Sibut, Paul and Etiennette began making arrangements to get married. The end of that week sounded good to them. Excitement swept through the mission station. Etiennette had dreamed about the wedding many times, but now everything was happening quickly!

"So you see, Monsieur, we're going to be married in a few days. What requirements do you have in this part of Africa?"

Paul finished his story with a broad grin and a wink at his fiancée, then returned his attention to the local government official sitting before him.

I was young once, too, the official thought with a grin. He sighed and glanced away from the young man's gaze.

"I cannot endorse your marriage until the official record book arrives. It is in Brazzaville now," he paused briefly, "but I am sure it will be here within a week."

The Frenchman had hoped to be encouraging with that last remark, but Paul knew that the mail porter stopped at each village along the way to visit with friends and relatives. Who could tell when he might get there? Paul's smile faded and his shoulders sagged. Etiennette caught the drift, and her bubble burst. Now what? They thanked the official and trudged back to the mission station to postpone their plans.

Two days before the new wedding date, the government official sent word that he had sent a telegram to Bangui to check on the book's progress. The book was on the way. Spirits soared!

The morning of the big day, however, the mailman sent a devastating note. He was terribly sorry, but the book was not in his mailbag. He guessed that it must have accidentally been put in the bag going to Bambari.

Bambari! Oh no! That meant another ten days' delay.

Finally one day a messenger came panting up to the station. The book had arrived! The wedding could take place the next day! Praise the Lord!

"And where are your white shoes, Paul Metzler?" the missionary ladies demanded.

"White shoes?" he managed to reply amid the scurry of last-minute wedding preparations.

"Yes, white shoes. They go with your white suit. It's tradition here. Didn't you know that?"

Paul slowly paid attention.

"I guess I'll have to do without," he shrugged. "I don't own any."

"What?" the horrified ladies exploded. "You can't possibly get married without them. We'll find you a pair."

"Oh, I have a pair you may use." Margaret Nicholl came to the rescue.*

Now everything was ready.

Early the next day the prospective bride and groom and their two witnesses dashed down Sibut Hill, jumped onto the waiting push-pushes and bicycles, and raced to the government building. The town's entire white population of two men and one woman joined the

---

*She later became Mrs. Margaret Laird, the author of *They Called Me Mama,* Moody Press, 1975.

beaming group for the civil ceremony required by the French government. As soon as they could get away, the wedding party hurried back to the mission station for the religious ceremony.

One of the push-pushes broke down on the return trip, so the new groom had to walk the last mile or so in his borrowed white shoes. They were not made for walking on rough gravel, so they pinched his feet mercilessly. Oh, how his feet ached by the time he reached Sibut Hill.

Boom!

Boom!

Boom! Boom! Boom!

One of the missionaries vigorously beat on a tom-tom as the wedding party ascended the hill. What a strange wedding march!

Brilliant orange blossoms fresh from the station orange grove filled the air with sweet fragrance. The Reverend Gust Pearson, a companion on Paul's trip to Africa, performed the ceremony as the bride and groom stood beneath a French and an American flag arranged on the enclosed veranda.

CHAPTER

7

Life in colonial Africa is hard, nearly claiming the life of the new baby girl.

A few short days after the wedding the newlyweds started out in their push-push for Fort Crampel. The new Mrs. Metzler leaned back and sighed. Here she was, thousands of miles from home, following her husband farther and farther into unfamiliar territory. She smiled to herself. Many romance books did not promise as much excitement.

She pulled her sun helmet down on her forehead a little more and slapped at a fly. The gentle sway of the push-push could even be relaxing. She yawned. The sun wrapped her in a cozy blanket, and the rhythmic whirr of the wheels did the rest.

Ugh!

The push-push had stopped short, throwing its rider forward. Etiennette sat up, blinking, and pushed her helmet out of her eyes. Were they there already? No, Paul's push was up ahead. Well, then, what in the world—and then she saw him.

She blinked hard, but when she opened her eyes again, he was still there in his push, grinning at her. He had to be someone important with all those medals.

"Good morning, Madame," he greeted her. "I am the government administrator for Fort Crampel."

Government administrator? Etiennette blushed.

"Oh, pardon me, Sir."

She was fully awake now, straightening her clothes and tucking in a stray curl. What must he think?

To her relief, he directed his push on up by Paul's, and then left them altogether. Somehow Etiennette did not feel a bit tired now.

A few hours later the newlyweds pulled into Fort Crampel. Then Mr. and Mrs. Young came hurrying over to greet them.

"I'm so glad you're here," Mrs. Young said, squeezing Etiennette's hand. "No matter how much I love it here, it gets pretty lonely without someone to talk to. A woman, I mean."

They fell into step together.

"Someone from 'back home' who thinks like I do. We'll have lots to talk about as you adjust to life here. It's not France."

"So come on," Paul interrupted, grabbing Etiennette's arm. "I took a little time out of my busy schedule as a devout missionary to fix up our very own place."

He directed their steps as he talked. The Youngs hung back, trying to hide their amusement.

"And here it is," he waved toward a small mud building. "Terrific, huh?"

Etiennette stared at it. Terrific? Compared to what? She glanced at her new husband. He was serious. She managed a smile as he pulled her inside.

The roof rested on a huge post exactly in the middle of the house. She could see it now: she and Paul seated on one side of that post and a guest on the other. They had to lean to one side to talk or pass the tea. If they forgot to lean, they would end up talking to the post.

It certainly was not her dream house. Well, maybe a woman's touch would make it more comfortable than it looked. She whispered a prayer, squared her shoulders and took another look around.

"Well, it is clean and neat," she thought aloud.

"Boyfini gets credit for that," Paul said.

As if on cue, a Chadian stepped forward.

"This is our houseboy. He's been pretty anxious about your arrival. He wanted everything to suit you."

Etiennette smiled at him and took the few steps into the kitchen.

"Where do you keep the water?" she asked.

"Here, Madame." Boyfini proudly pointed out the two metal pitchers on top of a tall dresser. "We will not knock them over up there."

Of course not, she thought. No one can reach them. We will have to find a more practical place for the water.

She leaned on one of the homemade chairs.

"It's not fancy, but it's sturdy," Paul said, still smiling proudly.

She glanced up at him, and gasped. Behind him on a small table sat a pair of his black shoes. Right on the table. She quickly stepped over and set them on the floor. She would have to explain a few things to Boyfini.

"I even had the walls whitewashed," Paul boasted as they walked back outside.

She smiled and nodded, then reached over and lifted the grass curtain hanging over one of the windows.

"There's no windowpane," she said.

"That's it," shrugged Paul. "Grass curtains do just fine out here. Hey, I almost forgot," he grinned, unmindful of the windows.

He put his arm around his new bride and led her to the corner of the house.

"We could even plant some flowers over here. Make it more homey, don't you think?"

Etiennette stared at the little plot of ground. No windowpanes? Not even screens or shutters? Those definitely were hyena cries she had heard on the road from Sibut. What would keep the creatures from climbing in their window some night? She shuddered.

The business of settling in crowded out these thoughts for the next few days. Then late one night they heard the hyena's eerie laugh.

Heeheehawhawheeheehaw! Heeheehawheeheehawhaw!

Etiennette's eyes flew open. She leaped from her cot to Paul's.

"Ugh!" He jerked awake. "Oh. Hi, Honey," he mumbled and lay back down.

"Thought the roof caved in or something," he teased the next morning.

"Did you hear it?" Etiennette turned to the Youngs. She still could feel the tingling in her spine. "It was just under the window."

"We heard the animals every night our first several months here," they smiled, "but they pretty much leave you alone if you have your door closed and your little grass curtains down."

Etiennette shuddered again despite their nonchalant manner. She silently asked the Lord to post an angel at each window.

A few nights later Paul tossed and turned.

"Oh, Honey, cut it out," he mumbled. He pulled up his knees, but that did not help. "Come on, that's enough," he said crossly as he sat up.

Etiennette still lay sleeping. Who would have been tickling him, then? He rubbed his eyes and looked again. Army ants! They were everywhere.

"Etiennette!" he shouted as he hopped out of bed. "Wake up! Quick!"

He nearly dragged her out.

"They can have anything they want till morning," he declared, building up the fire. Then he set two chaise lounges near enough to the fire to keep the ants away.

"Even a window wouldn't help this time, Dear," he smiled wryly. "Good night."

The newlyweds established their work routine at the station as soon as possible. Their days started early so they could rest during the afternoon heat.

One morning as Etiennette returned home from a ladies' class, she noticed that Boyfini had hung out the wash. Good, she thought, he must be quite efficient. When she rounded the last bend in the path, the clothesline loomed in front of her.

"Oh no!" she gasped in horror.

There on display was every piece of clothing Etiennette had brought to Africa, including her night gowns and underthings. Madame marched in the house to find Boyfini.

"Yes, Madame," he proudly explained. "This past year I had only men's clothes to hang up, but now I can hang out a lady's clothing. Now I will be accepted by the other missionaries' houseboys. They have had ladies' clothes all along."

Etiennette stared in disbelief as the young man strutted away. What a strange way of thinking, she thought. There is much to learn about these people.

A few months after the Metzlers settled into Fort Crampel, the Youngs left for a furlough in the United States. Soon Etiennette's health began to suffer. Must be the added stress of working without them, she decided.

"Oh, Paul," she threw her arms around him one afternoon when he came home.

He laughed and gave her a kiss.

"You must be feeling better."

"A little," she admitted, "but listen. We are going to have a baby."

A baby? He grinned and gave her another squeeze.

"But—" she suddenly became serious and took a deep breath. "I never had a baby before. What if I have trouble? Even mothers in France have trouble sometimes. The doctor is a hundred miles away. What if he cannot get here in time?"

"Well." Paul thought for a minute. "Hey, isn't Laura Bayne, that nurse who came with you to Africa, working at Bangassou? Maybe she could come."

Etiennette squeezed his arm.

"I think I will write and ask right now."

Several months later a messenger came peddling into the station. Mrs. Bayne would arrive that evening, bringing Mrs. Rowena Becker, another missionary with her.

"Oh good," Etiennette sighed and sat down. "It will not be long now."

Paul came over to hear the news. His face lit up.

"That close? Think I'll ride out and meet them."

When he saw them, he waved and reined his horse in to a trot. No need to kick up too much dust.

"Balao!" ("Hello!") he called.

"Balao," they returned. "How's Etiennette?"

He started to tell them, but they held up their hands.

"Whoa! In English, please."

He tried, but Paul could not seem to get any English out. After a year of only Sango or French his tongue must have forgotten. The ladies had to wait for more information until they reached the station, and Paul had to practice for a week to recover his English.

"Where is that government doctor?" Rowena Becker exclaimed as Etiennette went into labor. "You did remember to send a messenger, didn't you, Paul?"

"Yes. Maybe he's on his way."

Etiennette interpreted for him.

"Well, doesn't look like the baby's going to wait."

Laura Bayne rolled up her sleeves and put the others to work. There was no sleeping that night. Where was that doctor? Paul wiped the perspiration from Etiennette's face.

Another sleepless night, and still no doctor. Forty-eight hours passed. Suddenly new energy surged through them as the baby girl squirmed her way into the world.

"Paul, go take a nap," Laura Bayne waved him away. "They're both fine now."

The new daddy dropped onto his cot at eleven o'clock that morning. When he awoke it was noon. He quickly cleaned up and rejoined the ladies.

"Balao," he said as he strutted in. "An hour's sleep, and I'm rarin' to go. Pretty good, huh?"

Etiennette interpreted, and the ladies broke out laughing. Poor Paul frowned.

"Oh, it's been an hour all right," they snickered, "plus twenty-four. We'll just call you Rip Van Winkle."

After the ladies left, Paul and Etiennette tried to settle back into a routine, but they kept running into questions. Now that they had little Hélène, what were they going to do with her? If only the ladies could have stayed longer!

A few days went by, and the baby did not gain weight. Maybe she needed extra milk. Crampel had no cows, so Etiennette ordered condensed milk from Bangui. Hopefully it would arrive within the week. For now Paul asked a Christian national for some of his goat's milk.

Etiennette mixed up a Lysol solution to wash down the goat's udder and the milker's hands each time he came, and then had him fill a small bowl just half full. Without refrigeration she could not afford to keep any leftovers. She took the milk inside, poured it into a sterilized bowl and then fed Hélène a few spoonfuls. A little at a time seemed to be best.

Instead of growing stronger, however, little Hélène became terribly sick. What could be wrong? Paul and Etiennette prayed desperately for her. Mrs. Rosenau from Fort Sibut decided to come nurse the Metzler baby along with her own. The condensed milk arrived about the time she did, and they abandoned the goat's milk.

Much later Etiennette read that the goat's milk should have been diluted to one-third the original strength for such a small baby. Praise the Lord He had protected Hélène despite her young parents' lack of knowledge!

When the baby was two months old, she again became sick, and the new parents took turns caring for her day and night. They put the baby's basket on a chair close to their cots and made a mosquito net large enough to cover all three. They kept a lantern lit all night.

One day Hélène could not keep anything down and moaned constantly. Etiennette checked her temperature. One hundred five degrees! The next day the exhausted baby just slept, eating very little. Paul checked her temperature. Normal. The fever came back the next day and left again the following morning. The same symptoms continued to alternate days, and the baby lost the weight her parents had struggled so hard to help her gain.

One night little Hélène stopped moaning. Etiennette grabbed the lantern and peered into the basket.

"Paul! Paul! Wake up! Help!"

Paul sprang up. Hélène's head was completely black. He pushed the lantern closer. Hundreds of tiny black ants were sucking up the oil Etiennette had rubbed on the night before. More still marched up the chair leg to the feast.

Paul jerked up the baby by her feet and whisked the ants off with his other hand. The ants darted over her eyes and into her nose and ears.

"This time I know it is of the Devil!" Etiennette burst out.

Paul put his daughter down and turned to comfort his wife.

"Oh, Honey, you're just exhausted," he soothed. "You're not quite well yet from having the baby, and we've been under a strain with her so sick. You know we've prayed about this. Why don't you just lie back down now?"

Paul changed Hélène's bed, then he brought a basin of water and bathed her to bring down the fever. He did this every few hours the rest of the night, with Etiennette pitching in to help after a few hours' rest.

Several weeks later the baby was so weak it seemed only a matter of time before she would die. In their family devotions Paul began asking the Lord that His will be done even if it meant He would take their little girl. Etiennette could not quite bring herself to do that.

"Come on, Honey," Paul urged. "Why don't you tell the Lord it's all right to take her if it's His will?"

"All right, I will do it," his wife replied.

She knelt to pray, but all that came out was, "Lord, it would be a great testimony to the Africans if You would heal her."

Having to stay up all night with the baby did have a few advantages. By the time Christmas Day arrived Etiennette had had time to prepare plenty of prizes made from safety pins, buttons and pictures. Paul took them down the hill to the Christmas program that substituted for the ungodly celebration in town. All the houseboys eagerly ran down the hill, too, to join in the fun, but Etiennette remained behind with the baby for the afternoon.

She was holding Hélène on her lap when suddenly the baby's eyes rolled back and her little hands clenched into fists. Frightened, Etiennette could only think that her baby must surely be dying—and she had not yet even told the Lord that she was willing for Him to take her!

"Lord, wait until I have the chance to give her to Thee myself," she begged as she put the sick child back to bed.

In tears, she knelt by Hélène's basket and finally unburdened her heart, telling God what she had wanted to tell Him for a long time.

"Thy will be done."

The burden Etiennette had carried the past month lifted. She knew that, although the Lord would take Hélène, both she and Paul wanted His will and would grow closer to Him than ever before. What a relief! She busied herself with household duties and even found herself singing praises to God.

When Paul came home from the Christmas party, he froze halfway through the doorway.

"What's happened?" he demanded. "Hélène's not moaning."

Startled, Etiennette listened too. Silence. She took a deep breath.

"Come to think of it, I have not heard her moan since I put her back to bed a few hours ago."

They ran to the basket, fearfully peering in. Hélène was sound asleep and looked more rested than she had ever looked before. Paul gingerly felt her wrist—it was cooler than it had been that morning. With mounting excitement they took her temperature. Only 104 degrees! Praise the Lord!

"When Hélène was not moaning I thought the Lord had taken her," Etiennette said. "I talked to the Lord today. I guess it was the hardest thing I have ever done. But she is still alive, and even the fever is down."

As they watched that evening, the baby's temperature slowly but steadily dropped, and she never moaned again. By the next morning the fever was gone for good. The Lord had given their baby back to them, so the grateful parents dedicated her to Him for whatever life He chose for her.

As a result of this experience with their first child, Paul and Etiennette learned that all of their children would belong to God and be only lent to them. Would He let them all live? Would they be healthy? The parents did not know, but they did know that their Lord would act according to His perfect purpose.

CHAPTER
8

**Chad finally opens to missions, and
Paul leads an exploratory expedition.
He moves his family
to this wilder area.**

The Youngs and then the Metzlers worked to build up the church at Fort Crampel, and the Lord blessed. Every Sunday scores of people walked the three miles from the government post to worship. The chapel could hold only three hundred, so several women carried their stools on their heads and sat outside the windows.

Paul started first one and then several baptismal classes to teach new converts what it really means to be a Christian. He wanted to have believers truly understand their faith so they could live it. What good was it to report hundreds of conversions if the people did not take a stand for Christ?

After some months of instruction, a candidate for baptism would meet with the national deacons and the missionary. Often the missionary would have passed the candidate because he or she knew all the answers, but a deacon would disagree.

"The words of your mouth are satisfactory," he would concede, "but the words of your life are not. You cannot walk two ways at the same time. When you show that you have left the way of paganism and superstition, we will approve your baptism."

This strictness did not repulse the people. Sixty to seventy new Christians followed the Lord in baptism and then joined the church practically every month. Soon this church was sending pairs of its deacons on preaching tours down the roads that led in every direction. Some of these deacon-preachers later went to the Bible School the Mission organized and faithfully served the Lord for many years.

Chad opened to missions in the first few months of 1925. Paul and another missionary started right off for Fort Archambault (now Sarh), the capital of Chad. They wanted to get permission for a station and explore possible sites.

Usually ten days traveling by push-push would wear out anyone, but on this trip the men hardly noticed. Every time they stopped in a village and asked the chief if they could hold a service, he seemed to be expecting them. He gave the signal to the drummer, and:

Boom! Boom! Boom-boom! Boom! Boom! Boom-boom!

The people dropped what they were doing to come.

About halfway to Fort Archambault the missionaries stopped quite early in the morning. The old chief set his stool right in the front row.

"And so Jesus Christ was crucified for your sins because He loved you," Paul preached. "Just believe that His sacrifice will pay for your sins, and you can have forgiveness."

Tears trickled down the chief's wrinkled cheeks as the sermon ended. He stood up and all eyes shifted to him.

"Last night as I lay on my mat," he began slowly. "I wondered if there was a god somewhere who cared something about me. Many times I have looked up and down this road to see if someone would come and tell me something about this kind of god. The tears you see are tears of joy because I know that the one true God does love me."

Paul and his companion were tempted to stay there and teach the people. They seemed eager to learn, but the missionaries had to press on. When they arrived at the capital, they sought out the sultan of the country.

"And so those are our plans," Paul explained, unable to hide his excitement. "Is it all right with you if we go ahead and set up the station here in Fort Archambault? It's a strategic location to reach villages throughout the southern region."

"Your plans seem fine, just fine," the sultan nodded with a smile. "You will need guides to help you find a good place. I will send a few with you."

"Yes, that will be a big help," Paul responded. "We need to get the French administrator's approval first, but we'll be back this afternoon to go scouting if that's fine with you."

"No, no, no," the administrator vigorously shook his head. "You cannot build your station here in town. Go somewhere else."

No amount of persuasion helped. The missionaries were disappointed, but their guides did know of other potential sites. They settled for some acreage near the little village of Balimba on the banks of the Bahr Koh River, only five kilometers (three miles) from town.

In March 1925, the Metzler family, Walter Ganz and Miss Tillie Burkey started out to establish a permanent mission station at Balimba. It took about thirty porters to carry the missionaries' belongings, and they rented a barge for the load of lumber and building materials bought from a trading company. Several national Christian families came along to help.

These pioneers stayed in the government rest house in Balimba for a week while they worked on a temporary house. It soon became evident that even a temporary house would take more time to build than anticipated, so the Christians began praying for a way to move onto the mission site right away. The Lord provided a tent through an English explorer, and the group made the move. Actually, the tent itself could hold only Tillie's bed with just enough room left for the Metzler infant's basket. The others had to sleep under the overhang. They praised the Lord that it was the dry season and would not rain for several months.

Wild animals took advantage of the nice weather to prowl near the mission station. Two men were assigned to keep a fire burning all night to discourage them, but they found it hard to stay awake. After a few nights they started sleeping more often, allowing the fire to go out regularly. Lions stalked about the perimeter of the camp. A few hyenas even ventured close enough to help themselves to bones the cook had thrown out.

Roar!

Crunch.

Crrrunch.

Roooaaarrr!

Etiennette bolted up in bed.

"Paul, Paul! Are you awake?" She shook him violently. "Wild animals are coming! Shoot your gun to scare them away!"

With one hand groping for the rifle by his bed, Paul slowly pulled himself to a sitting position. He yawned, barely opening his eyes to shoot. Then he dropped back on the pillow and started snoring again.

His poor wife clung to her pillow. She could hear creatures scurrying away from the camp, but would they come back tonight? The next evening she demanded a rifle to keep by her own cot. She would even learn to shoot it if she had to.

During the day hired workmen helped the men who had come from Fort Crampel scour the forest for necessary logs, grass and bark to build the temporary house. It was nearly complete when they discovered that building a secure dwelling in sandy Balimba required larger poles that had to be sunk twice as deep into the ground as was needed in the rock country of Fort Crampel. What a time to realize the difference! The men had to pull down their work and start over.

When they had secured the foundation, they made rope from tree bark. Then they tied timbers up to six inches thick together to form the frame for a four-room house. They tied on grass mats for the walls and finished the job by making a thatch roof with several tons of grass.

No sooner had the missionaries moved into the temporary house than termites began feasting on it. Their steady gnawing often made it difficult for anyone to sleep. The missionaries rejoiced that they had a roof over their heads and could enjoy some privacy, but they urged the men to start work on the permanent building right away.

Each night after the missionaries had moved onto the property, the African families who had come to help gathered around the bonfire. The women put their children to bed close to the safety of the flame and then rolled out their own mats nearby. The men formed the outer circle, each with his spear beside him.

"Hey! He got him!"

"Oh no! He's gone!"

"Wake up! Go after him!"

Paul jumped out of bed and darted out of the house with his rifle just in time to see the last man disappear into the woods, spear poised.

"Boyfini! Come here!" Paul shouted above the commotion. "What's going on?"

"It's the hyena! They are after the hyena!"

"Hyenas prowl in the forest all the time," Paul countered impatiently. "Why all the fuss this time?"

He glanced around.

"Oh, the fire's out again. Did it come in close?"

"It walked right over the men and the women and picked up a boy," the story tumbled out, "and then tramped over everyone again on its way back to the bush. Someone finally felt its claws and then smelled it and woke up and screamed the alarm. Now all the men are on its trail to get the boy back."

Paul broke into a run.

"He was only nine years old," Boyfini called after him.

Paul slowed to a hurried walk as he entered the jungle that bordered the clearing on three sides. He had to keep alert in case the men had wounded the creature and it doubled back. Not far down the path he met the group returning, carrying the boy.

"Look at the boy's neck and face, Monsieur," one called.

Blood spurted out, spraying the men. Paul whipped out his handkerchief and pressed it against the torn flesh.

"Looks like the hyena had to drop him to get a better hold," he mumbled.

"It could have outrun us if it had grabbed a smaller child," one man declared as they hurried back to the station. "With a boy this size it could not run fast enough to get away. The hyena had to drop him."

Tillie Burkey, the missionary nurse, began preparing her own cot as an examining table as soon as she heard the screams. When her patient arrived, she dug in her medical kit for catgut and surgical needles. Paul helped her sterilize the instruments in Lysol and cleanse the wounds.

"Well, I wanted to be a doctor," he chuckled. "This is pretty close."

They had to sew up the gashes without anesthetic, but the boy did not cry out or even whimper. Christians prayed, and he healed quickly. Within a few days he was up playing with the other boys again.

The hyena remained bold, regularly stealing goats and chickens from the village nearby. Paul set a gun trap, which finally killed it. The villagers were so delighted that they celebrated all night, parading the carcass through the streets and chanting about its capture.

CHAPTER
9

Souls are saved while the newcomers build a house. Severe opposition spreads the gospel.

Mornings on the station at Balimba started early. Group devotions came first, then the men went to work clearing the land or building. Their wives joined women from the village for morning Bible classes with Etiennette and Tillie.

Many times during the day villagers walked miles through the bush to hear the "tene ndjoni ti Nzapa" ("the good news about God") from the white man's special book. They did not know anything about Sunday or about any other special time for meetings, so they just came when they could. Sometimes thirty or forty people, sometimes more than a hundred and sometimes a whole village would gather in the shade of a large tree on the property where Paul and Walter took turns sharing the gospel with them. A year or so later a chapel with grass walls and a thatched roof would replace the tree as a meeting place, and split-log benches would replace mats or stools as seats.

From the very beginning of the work, new Christians were encouraged to testify of their newly found joy to members of their families and tribes. Each Saturday different ones hiked to the outlying villages to teach lessons, which they had learned the day before.

They also wanted to invite the people to come to church on Sunday, but the tribal language had no names for the days of the week. The missionaries tried to help by introducing the French words, but the people preferred to make up their own designations.

Saturday became "La ti Bale" ("the Day of the Broom") because the workmen spent each Saturday afternoon sweeping up the compound. It had to look nice on the Lord's Day. Sunday became "La ti sambela Nzapa" or just "La ti Nzapa" ("the Day of Praying to God"). As these evangelists went out into the villages, they told the people that the first day of the week was the day to come to the mission station to hear the praying to God and the preaching of the Word. Many responded.

Construction of the station continued during the weekdays. The workmen started on the permanent house as soon as they found out about the termites in the temporary one. They knew they could not waste any time.

Stone proved to be scarce in this sandy region, so they had to make bricks. First, they used crosscut saws to cut planks to make the brick forms. Then they scouted around and found a very good type of clay about a mile up the Bahr Koh. Next the missionaries demonstrated how to mix clay with just the right amount of sand and then how to pour the mixture into the forms.

After drying in the sun, these bricks were stacked into the form of a kiln to burn night and day for five or six days, depending on the number of bricks in the kiln. Fuel for the first several kilns came from trees and their roots cleared from the land. The Lord also provided a large number of bricks from some kilns that had been abandoned by the government.

Now where would they get aged logs to supplement what they had brought? The men could cut down trees from the jungle, but they knew fresh timber is not good for building a house. One day Walter Ganz crossed the bridge over the river and saw a number of logs bobbing downstream.

"Hey, over there," he cried, pointing, "And it's a hard wood too!"

He spun around and darted back down the road the way he had come.

"Do you know anything about the logs in the Bahr Koh?" he impatiently asked the chief of Balimba.

"Yes, but what do you want with them? The government threw them in a few years ago and left them."

"Perfect!" he exploded, turning to go. He caught himself in time to properly thank the chief before rushing off.

"We'd like to buy the logs still floating in the river," he told the French government official in Fort Archambault.

"Why, of course," he shrugged. "We do not need them anymore."

Walter dashed back to the mission station to get workers to guide the logs as they rolled downstream. The Christians praised the Lord for preserving this timber just for them.

Two nights after the missionaries moved into the permanent house, a wind storm flattened the temporary one. The termites had eaten the strength out of the wooden structure, but the Lord had protected His people.

The French official kept putting off quoting a price on the logs he had sold them, even when the missionaries asked about it. Paul knew he really could not afford what the timber was probably worth. Some months only fifteen dollars in support came from America. He also knew the men could not have finished the house without those logs. The Lord had supplied their needs, and somehow He would get it paid.

One day the official came to visit the Metzlers in their new house. He had become a little less hostile to the work as he watched it develop. Paul again broached the subject of the logs. His guest fell silent, munching one of the cookies Etiennette had served. Then he brightened.

"This is the price," he said as he lifted his cup of tea. "The debt is paid."

Paul blinked. Paid? Already? The Lord solved that problem in a creative way.

As soon as they could, the missionaries began traveling to villages to hold meetings. Sometimes they would just go for the day, and sometimes they took several days and went from one village to another.

Paul wanted to be able to have his growing daughter along, so he built her a special push-push. It had a roof so Hélène did not have to wear a sun helmet, and two tiny windows where she could look out when she was sitting up. He was careful to make it long enough so that when she grew tired she could lie down and sleep.

"It looks something like a doghouse on a motorcycle wheel," Etiennette teased him.

Paul could hardly wait to take his little family to a village for services. The people thronged around him as usual, fascinated by these white people who were not French soldiers. When Etiennette stepped out of her push, the women jumped up and down.

"A white woman! A white woman!" they chanted, clapping their hands.

She was the first one they had ever seen.

Meanwhile, the men had arrived with Hélène's push. The proud mother lifted the little roof and stood her daughter on the ground. Hélène immediately tried toddling a few steps, still uncertain of her new skill. The crowd vanished. Hélène squealed and clapped her hands. The whole village was playing a game with her. Wide eyes peeked out from behind nearby trees or from hut doorways. The chief had backed up several feet, not daring to run because of his social status.

"What are you afraid of?" Paul asked him.

"We have never seen such a small white man before."

"That isn't a white man," Paul explained. "It's a little girl."

"What?"

Curiosity nudged the chief a little closer.

"Do you mean that white people get married and have children?"

He stared in disbelief. He knew about white soldiers and even white missionaries, but they were always adult men. Now all of a sudden here was a white woman and a white baby. Was it possible?

A few of the villagers edged in a bit to get a better look, and then a few more braved a step closer. When several had ventured from their hiding places, Hélène giggled and bounced toward them as fast as her little legs could carry her. Again they scattered, the toddler squealing with delight. She loved this game. Maybe the next village would play too.

Each trip the missionaries or national Christians made to a village produced interest in the gospel and in the other services offered at the station. Tillie created a dispensary, and Etiennette set up reading classes and worked to get a school going.

"You are doing well in class," Etiennette said smilingly to a quiet boy. "Will you be able to keep coming?"

"Yes, Madame." His eyes shone with pleasure at this attention. "My leg will take some time to heal."

Etiennette glanced down. She had seen several tropical ulcers in which the skin and tissues practically disintegrated into an open sore. Pus seeped through the bandages on the boy's leg.

"I will be able to come every day for months."

He smiled shyly. This was his ticket to learn to read and to hear about this Jesus Who loved him. He could hardly wait to learn the songs and Bible verses so he could take a part of this new world home with him.

One Sunday in church a whispered message rippled through the congregation. Several women quickly wrapped their shawls around their heads and slipped out the side door. What could be wrong?

The next day one of these women showed up at the dispensary. Tillie treated cuts and welts left by a rawhide whip. The woman refused to tell what had happened. A few women came the next Monday, and the next.

"When will one of you say what happens to you?" Tillie exploded one day when she had treated several for this same abuse.

"It will be worse if we do," one murmured.

Finally one of them burst into tears and sobbed out the story. They all came from another district in Chad. To crush a civil war, the men had been killed and these women given as wives to Chief Bezo, the government-appointed sultan of the Fort Archambault district.

"Every morning his soldiers take us to the cotton gardens. They have rawhide whips."

She shuddered.

"We work until sunset for him," another added, "and he gives us very little food. How can we stay strong to do this without food?"

What a relief to be able to talk about it freely.

"You have been healing my son's sore leg," one woman told Tillie. "He sang the songs for us and told us of your Jesus."

"We wanted to hear for ourselves of this God Who loves us," another chimed in. "Why would anyone love us? We are slaves. We have to hide in the bush Saturday nights in order to come on Sunday at all."

Tillie took the opportunity to share God's love with them again.

"Chief Bezo?" Paul exclaimed when he heard the story. "He's the one who sent guides with us on our first trip to help us find this place. He's always seemed friendly enough."

"Well, apparently he does not approve of his people coming to us except for medical care," Etiennette said.

"And sometimes not even for that," Tillie said.

"He called me 'Baba,' the term of respect too," Paul added, puzzled.

"Hey, Paul, didn't you say he was a witch doctor?" Walter piped up.

"You're right. Now that you mention it, he's the head witch doctor. His power over his tribe weakens with everyone who turns to the Lord and leaves superstition. Guess he's anxious to see no one does. We need to pray he changes his mind. We also had better pray for these women in the meantime."

Early in 1926 twenty of Chief Bezo's people came to see the Metzlers. "Monsieur, we are here to be baptized," they said.

"Do you realize your baptism will probably bring you more persecution?" Paul asked. "Are you prepared for that?"

"Monsieur, we have trusted Jesus Christ as our Savior," one patiently explained, "and we want to be baptized because that is what He wants. We know we will be persecuted, but so was our Lord."

Paul nodded. These Christians meant business. That was what the work here was all about. The next Sunday morning he baptized them in the Bahr Koh River, and several of them disappeared the following week.

Some time later the sultan of the town of Koumra, seventy-five miles from Balimba, invited Paul to come preach the gospel. He arrived in the afternoon while most of the people were still working in the gardens. He used the time to pay his customary visit to the chief, and then went to the rest house for supper. He spent the remaining few hours before the meeting in prayer.

Boom! Boom! Ba-ba-ba-ba Boom!

At least two thousand people answered the drums and gathered for the meeting, a much larger crowd than usual. Paul praised the Lord silently, and stood to begin. He always started by teaching a song, but these folks already knew it. They knew the next one, too, and the next one. This had never happened before. When he preached the gospel, the villagers even seemed to be familiar with it. How in the world could they have known?

"Has another missionary come through here?" Paul asked later.

Chief Belangar beckoned to a beaming young girl about sixteen years old. Paul recognized her as Chief Bezo's daughter.

"Nelimane!" he exclaimed. "How did you get here?"

"After I was baptized, my father would not allow me to stay with him at Fort Archambault," she explained. "He sent me away, and I ended up here. I am now wife to the chief's son. I hid my songbook and my Gospel of John and brought them along, and I have taught these people songs of Jesus and told them what I know about the gospel."

God had allowed persecution to scatter the believers and thereby to spread the gospel, just as He had in the book of Acts. Later Nelimane's husband believed and was baptized. His father begged Paul to stay there and start a mission station, but until other missionaries came to replace the Metzlers at Balimba they could not leave.

CHAPTER

10

The baby boy dies, and Paul becomes ill while on furlough.

In June 1926, Paul and his growing family began preparations to return to the United States for a furlough. God had blessed the work the three and a half years they had been in Africa, and now it could continue without them for a short time. They just had to challenge Christians to serve God in Chad. There were too many lost souls for so few workers to reach.

As the packing progressed, Etiennette frantically searched for canned milk for six-month-old Marcel Roland.

"Lord, please send us enough milk for the baby," she pleaded. "You know it takes nearly a month to get to Bangui, and there will not be any place to stop and buy some on the way."

The Lord never did send the canned milk, but He provided two cows.

"Thank you for not giving me my request, Lord," Etiennette prayed. "This way we have an abundant supply of milk that no one has to carry, and it is always fresh. You have thought of everything."

Paul rode out of Balimba on horseback at the head of the caravan. Etiennette and the baby bounced along in one push, and two-year-old Hélène peeked out of another. The cows and thirty porters stretched out behind, almost lost in the fading light of dusk.

They covered about twenty miles before stopping at a government rest house. Traveling at night was slow, but the dreaded tsetse flies swarmed in the daytime. No one wanted to take a chance of getting bitten and coming down with sleeping sickness, nor could they afford the death of the horse or cows.

Despite all precautions, little Marcel picked up dysentery before they reached Bangui. He grew steadily worse. As soon as the caravan pulled into town, Paul and Etiennette rushed the baby to the only doctor. He gave them some medicine just before they boarded the riverboat on July 13.

Even with the medicine, the baby died the first day out on the Congo River. If only that military doctor had had more experience with babies. Maybe they should have put off the trip until Marcel was older. If only . . . maybe. . . . The memory of Hélène's illnesses comforted the bereaved parents and reminded them that God did indeed know what He was doing.

The next day the boat tied up at the little town of Zonga just long enough to dig a grave and hold a funeral service. A French missionary who had lost his first child only a few weeks before preached comfort in Christ.

The Metzlers clung to that message even more when they heard that Paul's father had had a stroke. Already heavy hearts sank lower.

The little family transferred to a Belgian liner a few days later at Matadi in the Belgian Congo. When they were underway, Paul went below to take a nap. His bunk lay just under the cabin porthole, and when the ship turned, the sun beat down on his head. For the rest of the trip he was delirious. Sometimes he thought he was cuddling his dead son, and sometimes he mourned as though his father had also died. The ship's medical officer diagnosed malaria and gave him quinine shots.

Etiennette spent the rest of the voyage caring for her husband and daughter. What a contrast to her first journey on this river when all she had to do was anticipate a new life.

When the ship arrived in Antwerp, Belgium, waiting paramedics lifted Paul onto a stretcher and whisked him off to the ambulance. Etiennette and Hélène climbed in as well and stayed close until the hospital admitted the patient. Then a nurse suggested they go on home. Out on the sidewalk Etiennette clutched Hélène's hand.

"What do I do now, Lord?" she whispered. "I do not know anybody in Antwerp."

Gradually she realized that passersby were staring at them. What in the world could be wrong? She glanced down at Hélène. Oh, the sun helmets. Of course people would stare. She whisked off their tropical headgear and hurried down the street to a hat shop to buy something more appropriate.

"Could you please dispose of these for me?" She thrust the helmets at the astonished clerk.

Back on the sidewalk Etiennette breathed another prayer for guidance. Then she and little Hélène wandered down the street peeking into store windows. Suddenly a hand slapped her on the back.

"Why, Etiennette, what are you doing here?"

Startled, she spun around.

"Ted Wimer!"

The Lord had sent her another missionary of the Mid-Africa Mission. She clutched his arm to be sure her eyes were not playing tricks on her.

"Thank You, Lord," she whispered.

"We're serving in Brussels now, just a few miles away," he explained. "We had no idea you had even left Africa. Where's Paul?"

"He is in the hospital with malaria." What a relief to share her burden with a friend. "Where is a good place to stay?"

"Stay? Why, with us, of course. Lila will be thrilled to see you."

Etiennette gladly accepted his invitation. She could ride the train to see Paul every other day throughout his hospitalization. She thanked God for how well He had provided for them.

On Etiennette's first visit to the hospital, Paul's doctor met her in the hall to talk.

"Madame Metzler, your husband does not have malaria. He is suffering from sunstroke." The doctor knit his brow. "Unfortunately, his repeated injections have caused an infection in his right hipbone. He must stay here at least a few weeks."

Etiennette tried to hide her concern when she entered Paul's room. Week after week passed without much improvement.

"Do you have relatives you could stay with while recuperating?" the doctor asked.

"Yes," Etiennette said, "My parents live in southern France."

"Good," the doctor nodded. "I will release you in the morning."

By now Paul could walk leaning on two canes, but it was very painful. He barely managed the two days' train trip to Martrou. A local doctor tried several different treatments to relieve the pain, but it only grew worse. When it finally became unbearable, Paul went to the hospital.

"This man needs an operation right away," advised the consulting surgeon. "We need to scrape that infection from the bone. There is no time to lose."

The day after the operation the Mother Superior of the hospital came to visit.

"Monsieur Metzler, I am perplexed," she said. "I understand French, German, English and Italian, but I could not understand the language that you spoke in your delirium. None of us could. What was it?"

"Well," he replied thoughtfully, "I do remember dreaming that I was preaching in Arabic to a village near Fort Archambault. That must have been it." Then his face lit up. "Now let me tell you what I was saying," and he proceeded to give this Roman Catholic nun the gospel.

Twenty-four hours later the Mother Superior returned with a hypodermic of morphine.

"Thank you," Paul said, "but I'm not in pain just now. When I need it, I'll let you know."

The nun just stood there, stunned. Then she shook her head.

"In all my years in nursing I have never before had a patient refuse morphine. You are really perplexing to me."

Paul had his four-bed ward to himself for several days. Then one morning a local carpenter came in with a puncture wound in his finger.

That afternoon the carpenter threw back his covers and hopped out of bed. All six feet, two hundred pounds of him paced nervously up and down the ward, breathing heavily and cursing. He broke the drinking glasses and then grappled with the window in an attempt to open it. Could a rusty nail do this to a man?

Paul jerked the sheet over his head and clenched the call button in his fist. He knew he could not move with the drain tubes in his hip. Someone had to control this man. Soon nurses and doctors poured in. They wrestled the patient back to bed and tied him in. He died a few hours later.

Paul sighed. There had been no chance to witness. Now it was too late for his roommate to choose salvation. The priest came in to administer extreme unction. Paul sighed again.

After spending a month in the hospital, he went to the Lucs' home to recover quietly. Finally, in the beginning of 1927, the Metzler family continued on to America. They had been gone from Chad for seven months already.

Etiennette could hardly wait to see America. What would it be like? It was cold when they arrived in New York, and Hélène began to cry.

"What's the matter, Honey?" her daddy asked.

"My feet hurt, Papa."

"Let's see," he said as he knelt beside her. "Why, they're like ice. It doesn't get this cold in the Chad, does it?"

He rubbed her little feet.

"They'll feel better in a jiffy."

The toddler sat glued to the window as the train sped to Indiana. She did not want to miss a thing.

"Mama, feathers are falling down from heaven!"

"No, Dear, those are not feathers," Etiennette smiled. "That is snow. It only falls in lands that get cold weather."

In Mishawaka Paul's father was convalescing from his stroke, but he did not let that stop him from fixing a batch of mincemeat. He wanted a special treat for his guests. Etiennette watched, aghast.

"What in the world would anyone do with a mixture of raw meat, fruit and cider?" she asked her husband later that day.

"Oh, it's for a pie."

"A pie?"

Her eyes widened with horror.

"How could anyone eat such a thing? I know I will never get used to it."

She did eventually learn to enjoy mincemeat pie along with other new dishes that were served as the couple visited different churches. Most often, however, Paul was the one on the road, leaving his wife to feel like a "missionary widow."

The half-dozen independent Baptist churches in existence in the 1920s were scattered throughout the United States. Some felt they already supported as many missionaries as they could. They could not see the need of presenting another mission work.

Sometimes Paul attended one of the services anyway, to get to know the pastor and his people. In most cases he won an opportunity to present his challenge for missionary workers. Often the churches even became faithful supporters.

During this furlough Paul and Etiennette prayed long and hard about unrest within the Mission. Unhappy missionaries had been withdrawing and taking their fields with them. Mid-Africa Mission had desperately missed the Rev. Haas the three years since he had gone to be with the Lord. How could they generate his enthusiasm, spread his unifying love and reproduce his tireless leadership?

Paul met with his pastor, M. E. Hawkins, and E. S. Carman, the businessman who had helped start the Mission. They decided to work together to do what they could. Prayer meetings preceded reorganization meetings, and Baptist Mid-Missions survived. God provided new leadership, and the Mission started to grow again.

After only nine months the Metzler family returned to France on their way back to Africa. Paul's home church sent Miss Fern Minzey with them as a new missionary.

"I understand there is a new travel route from the coast of Africa to the Chad," Paul told the colonial officer in Paris. "It has to go through French Cameroun, doesn't it?"

"Yes, Monsieur. There is one planned, but I have no details about it."

The missionary hesitated a minute.

"Well, maybe I'll just go and check the way for myself."

Etiennette gave birth to Rachel Madeleine on October 17, 1927, seventeen days before Paul's departure date. He decided to leave his family while he went on ahead. One small grave in Africa was enough.

CHAPTER
11

**Paul leaves his growing family
in France on the way back
from furlough and leads
an exploratory expedition in Africa.**

A characteristic fine rain fell the day Paul left. A neighbor had brought over his two-wheeled carriage to take the couple the three miles to the train station at Rochefort.

Clip! Clop! Clip! Clop!

Would the horse ever get there? Their raincoats did not keep out the cold, and their umbrella could not keep them dry. What a way to spend their last moments together.

"The train to Bordeaux is several hours behind schedule," the station clerk told them.

"I am very sorry, Etiennette," the neighbor shook his head, "but I have already been gone too long from my farm. I have chores to do. Please, let us get going."

Etiennette squeezed out a reluctant good-bye and returned with a heavy heart. She felt so alone! She really did not know anyone from this village except her folks, and she bore the responsibility to care for two small children. She sank in a chair to pray.

"Lord, please help."

Soon the loneliness lifted. He Who had called her and led her thus far would lead her all the way.

Paul stood in the rain watching his wife leave. He did not know when he would see his family again. He sighed and turned toward his brother-in-law's apartment. Maybe he could find a way to kill time.

He walked around the living room looking for something to do. Over on a shelf sat a homemade crystal radio set. He pulled up a chair. Maybe he could reach a station he had not found before. Slipping on the headphones, he twisted first one dial and then another.

The speaker crackled. Paul twisted another knob.

Wheeeee!

He tried again.

Crackle! Whoosh!

Suddenly the static cleared and the chorus from St. Paul's Cathedral in London came in as if they stood behind him: "Fear not, I will be with thee; I will guide thee; I will guide thee with mine eye."

Then the crackling drowned out the music again.

Paul smiled.

"Thank You for that reminder, Lord," he said aloud. "I know You'll keep an eye on my little family."

What a relief to be able to leave them in such capable hands. Paul pulled off the headphones but sat staring at the radio.

"But you know," he mumbled, "after paying transportation and passage fees, I don't have nearly enough money for the trip inland. How—"

Suddenly he blinked and sat up. He chuckled.

"Well, I guess anyone who owns the cattle on a thousand hills can afford whatever He wants."

Paul boarded his ship in company with the Rev. and Mrs. Clarence Jeunnette. They stopped on deck to stare at the pile of identical trunks the hoist kept swinging aboard.

"Oh, it all belongs to a party of well-to-do Americans," a sailor told them. "They're going to Africa on a hunting trip, I think they said."

"A hunting trip, huh?" Paul mused aloud. "Well, I guess that's what we're here for too. That is, hunting for a quicker way into the interior."

His companions chuckled. Paul shook his head.

"These folks on vacation stay in first-class accommodations while we missionaries, on a mission for the King of Kings, stay in third class. What a backward world!" He sighed. "I wonder if they even think about God."

The ship pulled out of harbor the next day. Paul made it a habit to walk on deck each evening for exercise before going to bed. One night a smartly dressed woman took a few steps toward him. She hesitated, then took a few more steps. She paused again. Finally she took a deep breath and planted herself in Paul's path.

"Excuse me, are you a pastor?"

"No ma'am, I'm a missionary."

"Perhaps you can help me anyway," she sighed. "I know it sounds silly, but I'm afraid to go to Africa."

She gazed out at the endless ocean.

"I've read that people die from terrible diseases every day. And every year wild animals kill hunters and their parties."

She wrung her hands and shifted her weight nervously from foot to foot.

"I'm not ready to die. I'm even afraid . . . well . . . what if this boat sinks before we reach Africa?"

"Miss," Paul said gently, "there is One Who can take care of you here in the middle of the ocean, the middle of Africa or anywhere else if you'll only put your trust in Him. His name is Jesus."

"Oh, I was afraid you'd say that."

She knit her eyebrows as she sighed.

"You see, my father brought me up an atheist."

"But in spite of your father's teaching, you're afraid to die," Paul countered. "Why? Do you believe in a judgment after death?"

"Yes, I suppose I do," she admitted, then added slowly, "I'm alone in life and doomed in death."

Paul's heart went out to this lady. Her wealth made her influential in this world, but it could not buy her peace of mind for the next.

"Lord, give me the words to help her," he prayed silently.

"Look at this beautiful tropical night, Miss," he began. "You can reach up and almost pluck the stars from the sky. The same God Who hung these stars in place also controls the universe. But just think— He wants to be your own personal God, using His tremendous power to take care of you!"

"Oh, Rev. Metzler! How wonderful that would be! If only I could believe."

"Why not bow your head with me right now and ask God to give you the grace to believe."

The lady did so, shook his hand gratefully, and then hurried back to her cabin. The next day Paul met her again, but this time she smiled broadly.

"Rev. Metzler!" she called. "God answered that prayer and saved me! What's more, I slept the whole night through for the first time since leaving home! Believe me, there are many nights between here and St. Paul, Minnesota, to stay awake in."

The missionaries rejoiced together on earth as the angels rejoiced in Heaven.

Finally the ship arrived in French Cameroun. The next morning a tender would pick up the passengers who were going up the river to Douala. About ten o'clock that evening this newly saved woman came looking for Paul again.

"Rev. Metzler, you've traveled in Africa before, but my party and I are new to it all. Could you please come and answer some questions for us?"

"Of course. I'd be glad to."

The session wound down after a few hours, and the exhausted guest of honor excused himself. As he left the room, his new sister in the Lord slipped a check into his hand. He looked at it in his cabin. Two hundred dollars. In local currency that would come to . . . the blood rushed to his head. This would pay for his whole trip inland!

What God had wrought to keep His promise to take care of him! Ships left Bordeaux every week for Africa, but the Lord had brought this woman all the way from the United States, placed her on this very ship, put the need to know God in her heart, and then through her had supplied the needs of a missionary. Paul's heart burst forth in praise.

"What a God I serve! Thank You, Lord."

The next day the tender deposited the three missionaries with all their baggage at Douala.

"Yes, a road that will eventually connect French Cameroun and

French Equatorial Africa has been surveyed, but it has not been built yet," a local official informed them.

"Well, we bought a secondhand truck," the missionaries replied, "but if there's no road, we'll go ahead and sell it."

They hired transportation to Batouri, the last village on the existing road. They tried to hire men in Batouri to carry their baggage over the seven hundred miles of uncharted country still separating them from Chad.

"Sorry, all the men are busy working on the new road," a local official reported. "You can forget about hiring porters." He paused, then suggested, "Why not go on to Chad and send back porters from there? It looks as though you will need quite a few."

"Guess we'll have to," Paul said. "We have over a ton of hardware supplies to get inland, so we had better get going."

The Jeunnettes remained in Batouri with the baggage while Paul visited a local chief to hire a horse. The chief thought there should be enough porters in the very next town. Two days' journey sounded better than having to go all the way to Chad. The chief even rounded up five carriers to take some clothes, a bed and a food box.

Paul began the trip in high spirits, but ten miles down the path his horse lay down and refused to budge. He finally left it lying there and proceeded on foot. That would have worked out if the next town had really been two days' journey, but it turned out to be five. No one had brought enough food to last that long. At the end of the third day they grew weak from exertion and hunger.

The morning of the fourth day the group found a few palm nuts, but there were not enough to give much nourishment. The trail took its toll, winding up and down hill after hill, through ravines and across streams. The last day Paul could barely even crawl on his hands and knees.

"Lord, what can I do?" his heart cried out that evening. "I can't go any farther."

When he lifted his head he noticed a box. One of the carriers had picked it up because it was light. Only four porters had really been needed, so it had not mattered what the fifth man brought. Now it began to matter. What had he packed in the box? His weary mind slowly replayed the scene back in Mishawaka.

A little wagon and some other toys . . . yes, someone had brought them after the barrels were full, so Paul had just put them in this box. Was that all? He started to nail the box shut . . . wait, someone else came. Oh yes, Mr. and Mrs. Earl Kohli from First Baptist in Mishawaka. Now, what had they brought? A bag . . . a paper bag . . . a bag of . . .

of . . . of groceries! Paul's heart skipped a beat. Food! In this box!

Pushing himself up, he stumbled over to that wonderful box. He sank down beside it and frantically pried the lid off. He jammed his knife into a can of corn and a can of baked beans. Mmmmmm. Nothing could be better.

The next morning the safari finally reached the next town. Paul hired carriers from the local chief and sent them back to Batouri to get the baggage and the Jeunnettes. After several days some of the carriers returned with Mrs. Jeunnette in a tipoy (a traveling chair). Mr. Jeunnette had been held up with complications in getting the rest of the baggage through.

"We'll have to go on to a government post," Paul told Mrs. Jeunnette. "We can get food and supplies there. Clarence will have to catch up later."

They discovered a Swedish Baptist mission near the post and enjoyed refreshing fellowship. Paul used the extra time to make push-pushes out of motorcycle wheels he had purchased in France. They would make traveling easier during the rest of the trip.

"Well, it's been several days and still no Clarence," Paul said to his companion. "We don't have the money to keep buying food for all these carriers too long. We have to go on to the next town."

Several weeks later a stranger walked into their camp. He seemed to know them, but he did not look familiar. Slowly Mrs. Jeunnette began to wonder if this might be . . . was it possible? Could that shaggy beard be hiding her husband?

"I forgot to keep my razor," he laughed. "Just thought I'd see how long it would take you to recognize me."

CHAPTER
12

Etiennette follows Paul, they have a son, and new missionaries come.

The mailman came, and Etiennette rushed out. She quickly shuffled the envelopes, but none bore Paul's handwriting. She frowned, then more slowly read each return address. She sighed. It seemed as though years had passed since Paul had left. When would he write to tell her to come join him?

She turned and walked back to the house. She put the mail on the table, then sank heavily into an armchair. It felt good to relax a minute. Tonight she looked forward to a good night's sleep.

Too often she had awakened during the last few weeks to find baby Rachel turning purple. The doctor had warned that the whooping cough would not let the baby get enough oxygen, so Etiennette had slept lightly. Often she had had to shake the baby by the feet to force her lungs to exhale. Then the coughing started—the incessant coughing. Hélène had had it too, but now the girls went hours without coughing. What a relief!

After a few minutes Etiennette heaved herself up and dressed the girls. She had to keep their doctor's appointment.

"Ah, Madame, the girls are better," the doctor said. "They will be all right for traveling to Africa when you want to go. This nice spring weather will be good for them, but do wrap them up if it gets damp."

"Thank you, Doctor," Etiennette replied. "I was afraid they would still be sick when Paul wrote."

She sighed.

"But he has not written yet."

"Well, as far as I am concerned, you may go whenever you choose," the doctor said with a shrug.

After she had put the girls to bed that night, Etiennette wrote to a steamship company at Bordeaux.

"And the doctor has released them," she told the company. "We will be ready to go in a few weeks, so please hold tickets for us. Let us know the dates, the times and the total due. Thank you."

The company responded promptly.

"Thank you for your inquiry, Madame Metzler, but we believe you should stay home at this time."

Stay home? Paul has not written, and now even the steamship company does not want me to go back to Africa, Etiennette thought to herself. She could barely hold back the tears. She bowed her head and prayed for wisdom.

The doctor had said the girls could go. Maybe he would know how to get the company to sell her tickets.

"Of course they would say that, Madame," he explained. "If you had not mentioned the disease, all would have been well. Even now if you present yourself to the office of that company at Bordeaux and tell them that the girls have been sick, they will have no objection. They just will never commit themselves on paper. Remember, whooping cough is contagious."

The doctor's confidence flowed into Etiennette. She packed up and went to Bordeaux. The clerk responded as predicted, so Etiennette booked passage for herself and the girls and for Miss Fern Minzey from Paul's home church in Indiana. At least the waiting was finally over.

Etiennette sent Paul a telegram right away. She could hardly wait to see him again. The ship seemed to crawl. Although sympathetic, Fern relished the time aboard to practice her French. Language school could teach only so much. Practice was what made perfect.

When the ship finally anchored at Douala, a steamer brought friends and relatives from the mainland to escort the passengers into port. Etiennette and Fern stood examining every face for Paul, but he was nowhere to be seen. They finally could wait no longer to board the steamer. Had they somehow missed him as he boarded the ocean liner looking for them? Was he lost in this crowd?

After several hours they came in sight of the dock. Etiennette scanned the crowd for that beloved face. What would they do if he had not come? She spied a tall young African, vaguely familiar. She looked away, but her eyes seemed drawn to him. Wait, she thought as she studied him, he is not African after all. Who could he be? Then she gasped. It was Paul! Would this steamer never dock? After six months she could hardly wait to be a family once more.

"Where are the pushmen?" Etiennette asked when the excitement died down.

"Oh, they'll meet us in Yaounde. I'll fill you in when we get this baggage to the mission."

Paul had arranged with the nearby French mission to transport the baggage and to house them overnight. When they could finally relax, the little group sat down to enjoy the cool evening breeze and to exchange stories.

"I'll have to give Miss Minzey a little background first," Paul said, grinning at his wife. "You know," he turned to their companion, "I told her I would telegraph when she should come. But I was the one who received a telegram at the beginning of May. 'Meet me at Douala,' it said. That gave me less than a month to go the distance it took me two months to cover coming inland."

Paul winked at his wife.

"Women!"

110

Etiennette started to object, but her husband interrupted.

"Good thing I'd already made five pushes for us," he chuckled. "One for you, Fern," he nodded at her, "one for Etiennette and the baby, one for Hélène, one for me and one for personal baggage."

The baby woke up fussy, so Paul paused.

"So what did you do?" Fern prompted.

"The day the telegram came I asked our Chadian workmen for help. Their eyes nearly popped with fear."

" 'That is a long way, Monsieur,' one brave soul managed."

" 'What about the cannibals?' someone else squeaked out."

"Cannibals?" Fern gasped. "Here?"

She scanned the darkness around them, but her companions offered no sympathy. Etiennette sat singing the baby to sleep, and Paul had already continued his story.

"And I scolded them for such a lack of faith," he was saying. "We'd been praying that the Lord would send us new missionaries and would bring my family back, but no one was willing to do his part."

Paul sighed and looked up at the ladies.

"Just like in America, huh?"

"And in France," Etiennette added.

"And everywhere," Fern put in.

"Well, I encouraged them by explaining that the Lord had taken care of me and could take care of them, even on a trip," Paul picked up his narrative. "Finally ten came forward. As we left, their wives followed them down the road wailing, just sure that they would never see them again. I know it's hard on them, but they need to see the Lord work when He's the only One Who can help."

He paused to find a more comfortable position.

"We made good time reaching the beginning of the new road from French Cameroun, but I knew I had to make even better time if I expected to meet your ship. The Lord sent a truck along, going to Yaounde, and I caught a ride. I told the men to keep going and meet me in Yaounde."

Etiennette stopped rocking the baby to be sure to hear this part.

"They just stared at me at first. Then they asked who would buy food and protect them and keep them from getting lost. I reminded them that the Lord promised never to leave His children, and we prayed together. Then I left. I knew I had to get going if I expected to meet you."

"And we were afraid you had not made it," Etiennette cut in.

"Well, it was touch and go for awhile," Paul smiled. "I took the train at Yaounde and arrived in Douala at half past five the afternoon you arrived. The Lord had brought me on a two-month trip in less than one! Who would have thought it possible?"

Paul remained silent a moment before finishing.

"I rushed to the dock to wait, and the steamer came in at six o'clock. What a sight for sore eyes!"

"And we were awfully glad to see you too," Etiennette replied, smiling up at him.

Before long exhaustion caught up with the little group, and they found their rooms. The next morning they set off to meet the pushmen at Yaounde.

"How was your trip?" Paul asked. "Did you find enough food? Did you have any trouble getting here?"

"You were right, Monsieur. The Lord did not leave us," the words tumbled from one excited Christian's lips.

"At the first village where we stopped after we left you, we asked for food," another explained. "Before eating, we bowed our heads and thanked God for it as we always do. When we opened our eyes, we found others had bowed their heads with us."

"And when we sang hymns after the meal," a third broke in, "more people gathered about and sang the same tunes, but in their own tribal language. It happened over and over again in most of the places where we stopped."

"One man had a songbook from a Swedish Baptist mission," someone from the back spoke up.

"We never thought we could fellowship with other tribes who do not even speak our language," another added, "but they love the same God we do."

"And we thought they would eat us up!"

The missionaries rejoiced with the African Christians.

"Well, now, why don't you men rest here a bit before heading back," Paul suggested. "And please make sure you have all the baggage packed securely in the pushes."

The pushmen rested only briefly. They looked forward to their return trip and the chance to visit the Christians they had met earlier.

"Well, today I go to school," Paul announced after a day or so.

"What?" Fern frowned.

"Remember that Chevrolet truck chassis we pooled our money to buy?" he grinned. "Well, the poor thing needs a body."

"And you'd get that at school?"

"Yessirree," he chuckled. "An industrial school, that is."

Fern still frowned at his teasing.

"Here in Africa we don't just buy whatever we need," he explained, still grinning. "If we can get it, it's often more expensive than we can afford. So I'll build the body and bring it back to get you."

He did his work at a Presbyterian mission a hundred or so miles away, then hurried back to Yaounde for the others. They decided to take the nearly finished road inland to French Equatorial Africa.

At first they made good time. Then something went wrong with the motor, and the truck could hardly make the uphill grades. The Delco ignition system needed repairs, too, but even experienced mechanics could not locate the trouble. They simply were not familiar with the system since so few vehicles in Africa had it. Paul finally decided just to replace it with a magneto. He had to go all the way back to the coast to get the system while the others stayed in the government rest house in Batouri.

Finally Paul returned and installed the new system. The ladies gladly continued the trip despite its inconveniences. In order to cross some of the streams, Paul had to improvise bridges or rafts. Other places had makeshift bridges. He shifted into low gear to get all the power possible, and roared across. Little Hélène watched out the back window, hoping to see the bridge cave in. She giggled and clapped her hands when it did.

The Metzlers and Fern Minzey became the first travelers to drive a truck from the Cameroun coast into French Equatorial Africa. When they pulled into Bangui, people crowded around to see the first Chevy to join the few old Model T Fords in the area.

Back at Balimba Paul picked up the work where he had left off and once again settled down to a more-or-less normal family life. He liked to be able to play with three-and-a-half-year-old Hélène in the evenings. She often climbed on his knee for a hug, but six-month-old Rachel had to wait until he picked her up to get a hug. Could she really have been just two weeks old when he left for Africa?

"When she starts talking, I'll be in real trouble," he teased. "Three chattering ladies in the house. Woe is me!"

Weeks passed, and then months, and Rachel still had not begun to talk. She turned a year old before she broke her silence.

"Lo te kobe ti mbi!" ("He is eating my food!")

Etiennette choked on the water she was drinking. Paul's fork paused almost at his mouth, then slowly descended to his plate. He stared at the African boy who had been feeding Rachel. The boy turned around to face him, trying to think of something to say in defense.

"You know you get to eat later," Paul scolded the boy. "You can't eat my daughter's food too. I think you'd better go and not come back to work."

Rachel had been talking only three months when Edwin Harry was born early in February 1929.

The Metzler children grew up speaking Sango since they heard it all the time in Bible classes and church meetings. Also, nearly all Chadians used Sango to conduct their daily business instead of trying to learn each tribe's dialect. The children picked it up so well that sometimes they translated for their parents when bushmen came with unusual dialects.

In June Paul drove to Bangui to buy supplies.

"Gust!" he called when he recognized his old friend. "Gust Pearson!"

"Why, if it isn't Paul Metzler!"

The men shook hands and slapped each other on the back.

"And this is my wife," Gust turned proudly to the woman at his side. "We're going to Bangassou."

"Is that so?" Paul said. "My wife and I are up at Balimba, near Fort Archambault."

"Fort Archambault?" Gust repeated. "Let me introduce you to two young ladies who are on their way to Fort Archambault as missionaries. Well," he scanned the marketplace crowd, "they were here a minute ago."

"Over there," Gust's wife waved to the women.

"Paul, this is Ella Locken and Elsa Schlayer of Baptist Mid-Missions," Gust said when the women joined them. "Hey, isn't that the mission you're with?"

"Yes, it is," Paul answered. "Are the gentlemen with you too?"

Gust grinned.

"This is George Sinderson and Charles Shaw of the Sudan United Mission. They'll be passing through Fort Archambault on their way to Baladja."

"Sounds as if everyone's going my way," Paul said. "I have to get supplies, but then would you like to travel together?"

"Sure, thanks."

When Paul drove up with his truck loaded, the two male missionaries waved him over to their secondhand Ford truck.

"Bought it in the French Camerouns," George said, patting the hood proudly. "Has a few kinks, but she'll do just fine."

"A few kinks?" Charles snorted. "Just watch those brakes this time."

George laughed as he pulled out of town ahead of Paul. The veteran missionary quickly lost sight of the young people and would not have caught up with them at all if they had not gotten stuck on the bridge. Paul chuckled as he rolled to a stop. The Ford sat pinned between a truck loaded with cotton and the side of a narrow bridge.

The young people stared dumbfounded as the Frenchman in the other truck spewed out his contempt, his arms gesturing wildly. When he recognized Paul, he jumped down and stalked over to begin his tirade all over again. Paul managed to soothe his feelings long enough to untangle the trucks. Then the Frenchman gunned his motor and veered away, nearly spilling out the cotton piled on top.

The rest of the way to Balimba, the young missionaries stayed within sight of Paul's Chevy. George and Charles rested a few days at Fort Archambault before they had to go on to their station. Then they waved good-bye and hopped in their truck, but it refused to start. Charles sighed.

"Now what?"

George slid out and opened the hood. He and Paul leaned over the engine.

"Look at this," George muttered. "Distributor brushes. Worn out."

"Nearest Ford garage is over four hundred miles away," Paul grinned. "Time for some good ol' Yankee ingenuity. Etiennette, do we have an old toothbrush around?"

She found him one, and he made it into the part they needed. The truck did not know the difference and started right up.

One morning after they had settled in, Etiennette showed Ella and Elsa the school she had started.

"We teach all our subjects in French," she said as they walked around the schoolyard. "Chief Bezo terrorizes the villagers, but the boys keep coming. They are so hungry to learn."

They paused to watch the boys file into the classroom.

"Just about a month after school started, the governor general came to see it," Etiennette continued. "He seems satisfied that the boys are learning proper subjects and that they truly want to come, and he is glad that they are receiving instruction in the Bible too. He wants them to learn all they can."

About a month later Paul returned from a three-day preaching trip just in time to see a familiar Ford truck head down the road.

"Wasn't that George Sinderson who just left?" he asked his wife.

"Yes," she smiled, "he shared a report from his mission with us."

"A report?" Paul frowned. "It takes six days by push to get to his mission station. What could be so important that a messenger couldn't bring it?"

"Well, I am not sure," Etiennette replied, her smile widening, "but he carefully explained it all to Ella Locken there on the porch swing."

"Oh."

A knowing smile took over Paul's face.

"They seem well suited to one another," Etiennette commented. "We will see how the Lord leads them."

A few months later George joined the group who gathered for fellowship.

"I really look forward to relaxing in these cool evenings," Elsa said. "It's such a relief from that sun."

"In three or four months we will have to wear sweaters," Etiennette countered, smiling at her. "It will even feel cold."

"What's the matter, George?" Paul cut in. "If you grip that chair any tighter you'll pop a blood vessel."

"Ella and I have an announcement to make," the young man plunged in.

Ella studied her shoes, blushing slightly.

"We're going to be married during our next furlough." He gulped. "We'll be a missionary couple."

"That's great!"

"Congratulations!"

"Which mission is gaining a missionary, and which is losing one?" Paul asked, only half teasing.

"We're praying about that," George answered. "We'll have to see how the Lord leads."

CHAPTER
13

Another furlough but with severe heat and thirst. Back again, native Christians build a church. Paul becomes ill, and another work springs from that illness.

In 1930 the Metzlers decided to take another furlough, but they did not get away until after the rains had started. In several places the road disappeared under pools of water. They did manage to get a set of chains for the rear wheels of their truck, but even with this extra traction it took three days instead of the usual two to cover the less than four hundred miles to Fort Lamy.

They left Fort Lamy about ten o'clock one morning. The sun blazed between storms, driving the humidity higher and higher. Two half-gallon canteens with ten gallons of drinking water in reserve should have been enough until they reached Dikwa, English Nigeria, but the temperature edged past 120 degrees.

They seemed to crawl along. Here and there trucks had bogged down in mudholes, forcing travelers to detour. The children cried from thirst, and by evening the water was nearly gone.

"Paul, what will we do?" Etiennette asked in frustration. "It is hotter and stickier than we thought it would be, and we cannot seem to make any time. We will soon need more water."

"And there isn't any clean water along the road," he sighed. "Let's ask the Lord for an idea."

They bounced along in silent prayer for a few miles. Etiennette rolled her window up and rubbed her bare arms.

"Brrrrr!"

Suddenly she knew the solution and turned to Paul. He laughed.

"Yes, I can keep driving," he answered her thought. "This cold night air wakes me up and certainly doesn't make me thirsty. We'll let the children sleep during the day tomorrow."

"Just watch the road carefully," Etiennette reminded him.

She knew how bright the moonlight could get and how blinding it could be when it reflected off the dew. She also knew how quickly the dew came after the desert sun went down and the dry air chilled off.

They stopped to stretch their legs, and she pulled out some blankets to wrap around the children. Every so often she noticed a thin layer of ice on the mudholes they passed. What contrasts are here along the edge of the desert, she thought. It is so terribly hot during the day and so cold at night.

One night they slipped into one of the mudholes.

"Phooey," Paul spat out. "Didn't see that one."

He tried to rock the truck out, but only dug in deeper. He threw the gearshift into neutral in order to step out and see what he could do. Shortly he stuck his head back in, puffs of vapor chasing each word out of his mouth.

"Have to wait for some help. We'll have to set up camp."

He and Etiennette put the children to bed under their white mosquito nets. They set the gasoline pressure lantern in the middle so that its light could skip off the netting and dance in geometric patterns around them. Small pairs of glowing eyes emerged from the shadows around the camp, but the cowardly hyenas would not venture too close to such a strange sight.

Slowly Paul realized the voices he heard were not part of a dream. He hopped out of bed, breathing his thanks to the Lord. He followed the sound and flagged down the caravan to pull the truck out of the mire. Must be the Lord wants us to go back to daytime travel now, he decided. He yawned and crawled back under his blankets.

Whoosh! Flap! Crack! Hissss!

A violent wind had whipped up by morning. In places it pulled the mosquito nets out from under the mattresses and flapped them wildly.

"Hurry up!" Paul shouted, alarmed. "Get into the truck. We're leaving right now."

He dashed around loading the truck, but Etiennette protested.

"We cannot leave without breakfast. The children fell asleep before they ate last night, and I got up early to cook this oatmeal. Let them at least have that."

"Take it along," Paul shouted impatiently above the howl of the wind. "We can't stay. There's a rainstorm coming, and if it hits we'll be stuck here for nobody knows how long."

Etiennette knew her husband was right. The clay in these flat cotton fields could not absorb much water. A bad storm would make the roads as slippery as grease, and it would be months before they could get out. In fact, by the end of the rainy season this whole region would be under six feet of water.

The wind gave her a shove as if to emphasize the point. She rushed to gather up the children and the food and arrange room to eat in the truck. Paul sped along as fast as possible. He glanced in the rearview mirror and whistled.

"Would you look at that!"

The storm had already hit their abandoned camp, and the wall of rain chased them. At times it seemed almost to catch them.

At last their route veered away from the storm. The sandy ground in this corner of the Sahara drank in any rainwater, and the sun grew hotter and hotter. Once again the children cried for a drink. When the water ran out, Etiennette opened a can of evaporated milk.

"Ugh." Paul took a sip and wrinkled his nose. "This warm milk doesn't help my thirst."

"It is all we have left," Etiennette sighed. "We will have to stop at the next village and ask for some water."

"Alme mafi" ("Water, there is none"), replied the chief.

"You must have water," Paul disputed. "No one can live without water."

The chief shrugged his shoulders and spoke to his wife. She ducked into their house, returning with a small gourd half full of what looked like tea.

"This is all the water we have to offer you," he said. "We collected it after it rained many months ago."

They thanked him politely. He evidently had "collected" the water from the nearest puddle after it rained. The parents strained it through several handkerchiefs, but it was still too thick and smelled too bad to drink. They finally boiled up some strong tea and gave each child a sip.

Before they had driven many more miles, their tongues swelled and their lips cracked. The children whimpered. Paul drove at almost reckless speeds, but the town of Dikwa did not appear until five o'clock that evening. They headed directly for the government rest house to get out of the heat.

"Hello," Paul mumbled to the soldier in charge. "Please tell the official we've arrived."

He tried to lick his parched lips.

"And please apologize for me for not going myself as I usually do."

Instead of taking offense, the English official sent them several bottles of ice-cold soda water, a large dish of custard and several quarts of freshly boiled milk. Paul and Etiennette whispered a prayer for God's blessing on this kind man. They doled out spoonfuls to the children until they could stand more at a time. Later the official sent over a full supper, dish by dish.

When he felt the family would be refreshed, he came to see them. He even promised to wire the next rest house that a woman and children were coming, and again the family received thoughtful treatment.

The rest of the trip to America proceeded more smoothly. They really needed to rest this furlough, but it seemed as if they had just arrived when it was time to return to Chad. They carried back a new son as a special memento. Ralph arrived early in March of 1931, so he was several months old by the time his family boarded the ocean liner.

God honored the preaching of the gospel back in Balimba, and many trusted Christ as Savior. The missionaries organized a church to minister to these new Christians. Several young men and women offered their lives for full-time service.

"There are so many new members now; we think we should build a new church building," the deacons announced one day.

"All right, we'll help you make the bricks," the missionaries agreed. "In fact, we'll help haul in timber and bamboo, and grass for the roof."

"How big do you want it?" Paul asked.

"We want to be able to seat four hundred people."

"Four hundred? Why so many? You know Chief Bezo has stepped up his efforts against us, and some Sundays only you men and your families can come."

"Well, we thought we would build a large church and pray that the Lord will send the people to fill it."

Paul stared at them an instant, then smiled.

"Well, who can argue with faith like that?"

Work immediately began in earnest. When the building was nearing completion, Paul became extremely ill.

"It doesn't act like malaria, Doctor," Tillie Burkey, the nurse, reported.

"Well, I need hospital facilities in order to give an accurate diagnosis," the local French doctor declared, "and there is no hospital for hundreds of miles."

While everyone remained baffled, Paul grew worse. Sometimes Etiennette had to call in several workmen to hold him in bed because the pain had become unbearable. Finally, out of desperation, Etiennette and Tillie decided to take him to the Presbyterian hospital in French Cameroun for X rays.

"You will never reach the coast in time," the French doctor warned.

"Well, I'll sure try," Ted Wimer volunteered. "The Lord took care of this man's infection back when I worked in Belgium, and He will take care of him now."

The road through Fort Crampel to the coast had been finished by this time. It provided a fairly direct—if not speedy—route. At Bangui Paul suffered another attack, and only fervent prayer helped him survive to continue the other two thirds of the trip. The doctor at the hospital decided Paul's kidney was involved.

"You are very fortunate," he said. "I just received a sample dye from Germany. It is injected into the blood so we can get X rays of the kidney."

The diagnosis came back as strangulation caused by a floating kidney.

"Now at least you know the problem," the doctor stated, smiling. "Unfortunately, we are not equipped to perform the necessary operation here. You will have to go to France or America."

Ted Wimer sent a telegram to Fort Archambault with one word: "France." (It was closer.) He put Paul on a ship and then returned to the mission. Sad-faced Chadian Christians met them.

"Don't worry," Ted comforted them, "the Lord will take care of him."

"We know, Monsieur," came the answer, "but Chief Bezo does not. He has told everyone that our God cannot take care of the missionaries here. He has to send them back to the white man's country, and once they leave they will not come back."

"He is just trying to shake your faith," Etiennette sighed. "The Lord will take care of Paul."

"Yes, an operation certainly is imperative," the doctor at the American hospital in Paris informed Paul. "However, we need to have you here for observation for several months before we attempt it."

"But that's impossible," Paul protested. "My wife and family and my work are back in Africa. You operate, and we'll trust God to do the rest."

The doctor reluctantly agreed. A few days after the operation George and Ella Sinderson came to visit.

"So, how's life as a missionary couple?" Paul asked in greeting them.

"We like it better than being single missionaries," they replied, grinning.

"And to think it all started back on the Balimba porch swing," Paul retorted. "Are you studying French here in Paris now?"

"Yes, but tell us about central Africa," George urged. "What opportunities do you see for expanding the work there?"

"Well, years ago Chief Belangar gave me an open invitation to start a station in Koumra," Paul replied.

Then he proceeded to relate how Chief Bezo's own daughter had taken the gospel to Koumra when her father had driven her out because of her faith. George and Ella left, praying about this need.

When they returned to Africa in February of 1943 under Baptist Mid-Missions, they opened a work in Koumra. The church there grew to seven hundred members. They sent out more than forty preachers through the years to establish other churches and preaching points.

A four-year Bible school built later trained men from Fort Archambault, Balimba, Kyabe and Goundi. Because the Sara tribe centered around Koumra, Bible translation settled there. The Chad medical center also developed there, treating patients and training nurses and midwives.

None of the missionaries in Balimba ever expected such far-reaching results from a floating kidney. Paul just praised the Lord for allowing his painful predicament to produce such fruit.

Above: Dr. and Mrs. Millon, director of the Baptist Bible Institute of Bordeaux, France, where Etiennette and Paul met in 1922.
Below: The first chapel at Fort Crampel.
It could hold about 300 people.

Top left: Lilianne, Paul, Jack, Ralph, Hélène, Edwin, Etiennette, Rachel (1936).
Bottom left: Paul and Etiennette with missionary Clara Crum (left) and Lilianne (who went Home in 1938 at the age of six), Jack and Baby Evelyne in front of their home in Balimba.
Top right: Three Chadians standing in front of a cotton harvest.
Bottom right: On "La ti Nzapa" (the Day of Praying to God) believers were baptized in crocodile-infested waters.

Top: The missionaries opened their homes to French and English soldiers for Bible study and fellowship during WWII. Many of them later died on D day. The Metzlers worked with G.I.s in Bordeaux, France (1955-56).
Bottom: Paul Metzler graduated from Baptist Bible Seminary in 1949, after having served as a missionary for twenty-five years.

Top: Paul and
Etiennette with
their six surviving
children (1946).
Standing: Jack,
Hélène, Ralph,
Edwin. Seated:
Rachel, Paul,
Etiennette, Evelyne.
Bottom: Paul and
Etiennette
embarking from
New York. They
returned to Chad
after furlough and
a short-term
ministry in Haiti.

Top: Hélène Metzler served as a missionary nurse in Chad.
Bottom: During the 1950s the Metzlers served in France.

Top: All three ''Metzler girls'' became missionaries under Baptist Mid-
Missions. Here they say farewell at Balimba in 1966.
Bottom: Three delightful little girls from the work at Balimba (1968).

In 1968 the Metzlers dined at the White House;
in early 1969 they ministered in the Bahamas.
Soon afterward the Lord called Paul Home.

CHAPTER
14

Paul returns from the hospital in France when God gives the money, and native Christians build another church.

How soon may I return to Africa, Doctor?" Paul asked the week after his operation. "I'm feeling much better now."

"Return to Africa?" The doctor frowned. "We did not wait for observation before the operation, and now you want to run off so soon following it?" He shook his head. "Maybe you can go in two or three months. Not before."

His stern reprimand calmed Paul down for the moment, but three weeks later he made his reservation to return to the field. Then he wrote the Mission to send passage money.

"Newly elected President Franklin D. Roosevelt has closed all the banks," the home office replied, "and it is impossible to send any funds outside the United States."

First the doctor had said to stay put, and now even the president of the United States wanted to keep him out of Africa. Frustrated, Paul threw the letter on the bed. Then he sighed, spread it out, and knelt beside it.

"Lord, although the president has closed the banks in America, I'm sure You have not closed the banks of Heaven. Please help me get passage money. Thank You in advance. In Your Name, Amen."

Where would the money come from? He had no idea, but he knew the Lord had it all planned out. The following Sunday the pastor of a Baptist church in Paris asked Paul to give his testimony.

"And that's what God has been doing for us in the Fort Archambault area," he said as he closed. "Lord willing, I will be sailing for Africa next Thursday."

He made it a point not to tell them that he still did not have enough money to pay for his ticket. As he left the little hall where the church met, a man slipped an envelope into his hand. Paul waited until he reached the privacy of his room to open it. Three one-thousand franc bills! That would be three hundred dollars, he marveled, exactly enough to buy a ticket to the coast of Africa. The next day he looked for the man who had given him the envelope.

"Thank you so much," he exclaimed, pumping his companion's hand. "God used you to answer my prayer."

"Well, God wanted you to have that money," the man replied. "You see, several years ago I lent money to a fellow, but he had never repaid me. Saturday afternoon I was passing by his office on my way home and felt an urge to go in and approach him about it. He did not even wait for me to get all the way into the office. He just blurted out: 'I want to repay that money you lent me.' The banks are closed on Saturday afternoons, so I could not deposit the money, and so it was still in my pocket as you spoke of returning to Africa. The Lord seemed to tell me that you needed it more than I do."

"Thank You, Lord," Paul prayed as he sailed down the coast of Africa. "You gave me passage money just as I asked. Now I can hardly wait to see what You'll do to pay for my trip inland."

He still did not know how his God would provide as he boarded the surfboat that took passengers from the ship to the shore. While still half a mile from the port of Kribi, French Cameroun, he saw someone waving at him. Now, who knew him here? As he approached the dock, he recognized fellow missionaries.

"Margaret Nicholl—oh, I mean Margaret Laird," Paul greeted them. "Guess I keep thinking of you as the single woman who lent me shoes to get married."

"It's good to see you too, Paul," the Lairds replied, laughing. "Actually, we're sure glad to see that boat out there. It means a furlough to us."

"So what's new?" Paul asked.

"Well, we were wondering how to get our pickup back inland," Mr. Laird answered. "We borrowed it. Would you take it for us?"

Paul laughed.

"Of course. I wondered how the Lord would get me back home. He thinks of everything, doesn't He?"

The next day a steam launch came in to tow the surfboats back out to the ocean liner. Passengers bound for America climbed aboard.

"Would you like a hand keeping the children together?" Paul offered. "I have a little time to kill."

"Oh yes, thanks, that would be great," Margaret quickly answered. "You know how hard it is in these crowds."

The missionaries organized themselves on deck and finally started to say good-bye.

"Hey," Paul raised a finger to quiet the others. "Isn't that the engine firing up?"

He ran to the railing.

"Where's the launch?"

Then he saw it being hoisted aboard. Paul's shoulders sagged. The African boatmen in the surfboat below looked frantic.

"Those boats have no motors, and shore is a long way off," Paul sighed. "Guess I had better get going."

The boatmen strained on the oars, but a storm whipped up before they had covered half the distance to shore. The wind blew them back out to sea. Waves broke over them, so the men gave up their futile rowing to bail out water.

The sun slid toward the endless ocean in the west. Soon the only light came from a faraway lighthouse, and then even that disappeared. As his eyes grew accustomed to the dark, Paul realized the boatmen were taking off their clothes and tying them into bundles.

"What in the world are you doing?"

"Don't you see? The boat is going to sink," one shot back. "We want our clothes to drift ashore so the people will know what happened to us."

"Don't panic—we will be fine," Paul assured them.

He did not feel quite as confident about that as the Biblical Paul had in Acts 27. After a pause he added what he could be sure about. "The Lord has always taken care of me, and I know He will do so now."

The Lord nudged a song into his mind, and he began to sing:

Master, the tempest is raging!
The billows are tossing high!
The sky is o'er-shadowed with blackness,
No shelter or help is nigh:
"Carest Thou not that we perish?
How canst Thou lie asleep,
When each moment so madly is threatening
A grave in the angry deep?"

"The winds and the waves shall obey My will,
Peace, be still!"
Whether the wrath of the storm-tossed sea,
Or demons, or men, or whatever it be,
No water can swallow the ship where lies
The Master of ocean and earth and skies;
"They all shall sweetly obey My will;
Peace, be still!
Peace, be still!
They all shall sweetly obey My will;
Peace, peace, be still!"

By the time Paul had sung it through twice, the wind hushed and the sea smoothed out. Even the frightened boatmen joined in as they rowed the several hours back to shore. Paul knew that someone, somewhere, was praying for him that night.

"We thought we would never see you again," a shoreman told Paul. "The wind blew the roofs off several houses around here and uprooted trees. We certainly held out no hope for you in your light craft. Even the captain of that ship wired us wanting to know if we had found you or not."

"But you see, my God controls the wind and waves," the missionary said. "He still has work for me to do."

Paul drove back to Fort Archambault in four days. It felt so good to be home with his family and his work. The deacons came right out to greet him.

"We are so glad the Lord answered our prayers and brought you back," they told him. "Chief Bezo said you would not return, but you did, and you look better than ever."

"Those prayers brought me back," he replied. "You know, I've heard that Bezo has increased his persecution of the Christians. What happened?"

"He hid his soldiers along the bridge between Balimba and the mission," a deacon explained. "When people tried to pass, these soldiers would catch them, tie them up and take them either to the chief's prison for a beating or to work as forced labor in the cotton fields."

"But now everyone can see that Chief Bezo was wrong about you," another deacon cut in. "Lord willing, they will see how wrong he is to fight God."

One day soon after her father's return, five-and-a-half-year-old Rachel planted herself in front of him. Her little face wore a puzzled frown.

"Where were you born?" she asked.

"In Indiana, in the United States," he replied.

"Where was Mother born?"

"In Rochefort-sur-Mer, in France."

"Well, where was Hélène born?"

"In the Oubangui Chari district here in French Equatorial Africa."

"How about me?"

"In Martrou, France."

"Edwin?"

"In Fort Archambault."

"And where was Ralph born?"

"In Mishawaka, Indiana, like I was. Why are you asking?"

She heaved a sigh.

"How did we all get together like this?"

Her father swallowed his urge to laugh. He carefully explained that God puts families together no matter where they are born. In August when Lilianne was born, Rachel smiled knowingly at her little brothers.

"God is still putting our family together," she told them, "even if we are all mixed up when we are born."

Word spread quickly that Paul had returned. More and more people defied Chief Bezo and came to services. Soon seven to eight hundred overflowed the church built to seat four hundred.

"The Lord is so good!" a deacon burst out one day. "We need to build a bigger church."

"Yes," another agreed. "Some who have to sit outside go home when it rains. We need more room inside."

"Great idea," one of the missionaries encouraged. "But this time let's get all the Christians involved as well as you deacons and us. How big?"

"Oh, it should seat at least twelve hundred."

With everyone working together, even such a large project progressed quickly.

One day one of the African pastors threaded his way between the workers to find Paul and share his burden.

"Monsieur," he said, "I believe Bezo is sick and in hiding. I am going to find him."

"Sick?" Paul repeated in surprise. "He certainly won't want anyone to know."

"No," Congowa shook his head. "I went to talk to him about Jesus last week, but no one had seen Bezo for several days. I had to ask many questions. Finally I learned he had ordered a special hut to be built far back in the bush."

Paul shook his head.

"To have to hide so no one can see how sick he is!" he sighed. "You have been faithful in testifying to Chief Bezo many times, Congowa. We will certainly pray that you can find him and give him one more chance to accept forgiveness in Christ."

"Monsieur!" Congowa called out as he hurried over to Paul a few days later. "Monsieur, I found him! God answered prayer!"

Paul looked up from mixing cement for the church building project and wiped the sweat from his forehead.

"What happened?" he urged.

"I had to walk through blood up to my ankles to get to the door of his hut," Congowa panted out.

"What?" Paul wrinkled his eyebrows. "Why?"

"The sacrifices, Monsieur. Goats, mostly, but oxen too. He is a witch doctor, and he thought he was dying."

Paul shook his head and sighed.

"Could you speak to him? Did he hear you?"

"Oh yes, Monsieur. That is the best part."

Congowa's eyes grew wider.

"I told him, 'Bezo, you know that the blood of animals cannot forgive your sins and open Heaven to you. Only the blood of the Son

131

of God, Jesus Christ, can do that.' Immediately Bezo said, 'I know it. I have fought the white man's God, but He is stronger than all our fetishes.' Then he ordered the slaughter to be stopped and said he was ready to accept the Lord as his Savior. At last!"

Even the Christians who had suffered from the chief's persecution rejoiced to hear he was now a brother in Christ. A few days later Congowa reported Chief Bezo's death. Missionary Arthur Seymour led the funeral.

The Lord had triumphed over the witch doctor's power, had graciously saved the chief's soul, and had used his persecution of Christians to spread the gospel. The Christians had many reasons to rejoice.

CHAPTER
15

**Paul leaves his family in France while
he goes to the States to raise support
and recruit new missionaries.
Back in Africa, a daughter dies.**

Well, Etiennette," Paul began one evening, "are you and Fern ready to go on another preaching trek? I'm going day after tomorrow if you want to come along."

"That sounds good," the ladies answered. "We will be ready."

They visited a remote village. People pushed closer and closer to see the white women, pointing and chattering. Etiennette and Fern could not get through the crowd.

"Please tell everyone to go home for awhile," Paul finally asked the chief. "These ladies are tired from the trip, and would like to wash up a bit and refresh themselves."

"That is impossible," the chief shook his head. "No one will go home."

"Why not? We'll let them know after awhile when they can all return for a meeting."

"It is the ladies' hair," answered the chief. "My people do not believe that all of it is real. Perhaps if the ladies would take it down so everyone can see if it really stays on, they can be persuaded to leave."

Paul returned to the women and shrugged.

"This is one of the drawbacks of being so famous," he teased. "I guess the people think you borrowed some hair from someone else."

"I will never take down my hair in front of such a crowd," declared Etiennette.

"I don't like the idea either," Fern frowned. "It just isn't done."

Paul shrugged again, chuckling.

"Then you'll just have to enjoy your admirers."

Etiennette and Fern unpacked and arranged their things in the rest house. They pretended to be too busy to notice the faces in every window or the bolder ones who inched in the doorway little by little.

Etiennette finally sighed and turned to her friend.

"We might as well give in."

Fern slowly agreed. Etiennette called to Paul.

"Please tell the chief to make the people promise to leave us alone if we show them our hair."

Before the chief finished his announcement, the people began clapping and chanting in rhythm. Here and there someone burst into laughter. Fern and Etiennette looked at each other and took deep breaths. Then they slowly let down their long hair and backed toward the crowd at the door.

The villagers could not get over the fact that white women could grow their hair so long. Maybe these unusual people had an amazing God too. Curiosity brought scores to the meeting that evening. Paul preached about God's plan to forgive men's sins by paying the penalty Himself, but this baffled the people more than the hair had. Why would He care so much? The villagers decided this God was truly amazing. They would have to hear more.

The Lord sent Jack (Jacques) into the Metzler family in 1935. By this time Hélène and Rachel could help with the younger children. Evelyne came along in 1937, shortly before Hélène packed to go to America. The junior-higher needed to continue her schooling. That left Rachel as the oldest of the six remaining children.

"Well, cherie, the Lord has sent enough money to get us to France," Paul told Etiennette one day a few months later, "but not enough to go all the way to America for furlough. We need to talk about it and pray."

When the family sailed, everyone knew that Father would drop them off at Grandmere and Grandpere Luc's in France, and then go on to the States alone.

"I'll send money for your passage as soon as the Lord gives it to me," he promised as he gave his wife and children good-bye hugs.

She did not know how long it would be, so Etiennette enrolled her two oldest children in school. One morning they bundled up and headed out the door to school but stopped short on the steps. They knew things were different in France—for one thing they had to wear coats to keep warm in the middle of the day here—but what in the world had happened last night?

Poor Rachel and Edwin stood on the porch, too stunned to move or even talk. The yard was white, the neighbors' houses were white, the trees were white, the birdhouse was white and the bushes were white. Had someone plucked a cloud?

The youngsters carefully lifted one foot and then the other and began to pick their way through this new world. Each step took them farther from the safety of home.

"Are you sure we turn here?" Edwin finally broke the silence. "I thought we turned up there before."

Rachel squinted in the direction her brother pointed but shook her head.

"No, we turn here," she replied over her shoulder as she took another step. Then she stopped and sighed, "I think."

Where were they along the three miles to school? Did they turn here or up there? How would they ever find their way home again? What were they going to do?

By the time a group of French children overtook them, the two newcomers were too frightened to even follow them to school.

"Well, why not just go home then?" one boy asked with a shrug.

"That is a good idea," an older girl agreed. "Do you know how to get back home?"

Wide-eyed Rachel and Edwin shook their heads, so their new friends showed them. Safe inside, the youngsters spilled out their story.

"But why not just go on to school?" asked Mother.

"We can't," Edwin blurted out. "The road is gone."

Patient explanations helped the youngsters learn to cope with—and even enjoy—the snow. They also made friends with the French children.

"If you are from Africa, are you African?" a boy about Edwin's age asked one day. "Do all Africans speak French?"

"You are not African if your parents are not African," one of the oldest girls in the group retorted. "Where are your parents from, Rachel?"

"Mother is French, and Father is American," she answered.

Suddenly she realized she had everyone's attention and rushed on.

"We speak both French and English at home all the time, and Sango when we are in Africa."

Several pairs of eyes widened at this revelation. Their parents were French, they were French, they spoke French and lived in France. These newcomers seemed all mixed up. Oh well, they liked them anyway.

When Father sent the promised tickets, Rachel and Edwin said a reluctant good-bye to their friends. They met new friends and walked through snow again, but this time in France had been special.

Metzlers returned to Africa in 1938. A few weeks later Etiennette invited the French official and his wife from Fort Archambault to come for afternoon tea.

That morning six-year-old Lilianne and three-year-old Jackie came dashing in to "help" Mother bake the cookies. She gave them each some dough to mold and asked Saria, the houseboy, to bake their cookies for them. The children went right to work shaping that precious dough. That afternoon Lilianne complained of a stomach-ache.

"Too many cookies, eh?" Etiennette asked, smiling. "Lie down for now. You will feel better soon."

The guests came as Lilianne went to lie down. They stayed a few hours.

"You can get up now, Lilianne," her mother called.

"She doesn't feel good," Jackie reported.

Etiennette went to investigate. Her daughter had a fever that refused to come down. It could not be the cookies since no one else felt sick. Later in the evening Etiennette sent for the French doctor in Fort Archambault.

"No rum in the house?" the doctor chided. "Christians! I could have made an elixir to bring down the fever." He snorted. "Well, you had better take her to the hospital tomorrow morning, then."

The next day Paul and Etiennette rushed their daughter to the hospital. Her temperature topped a hundred and five degrees. By now the little patient was unconscious most of the time, but once she opened her eyes and looked into her mother's face.

"Do you love me?" she whispered.

"You know I love you," her mother squeezed her hand. "But do you know Who loves you more than I do?"

Lilianne managed a smile.

"Jesus."

Her eyes closed, and she slipped back into a coma.

During the first few days of Lilianne's stay in the hospital several Europeans who lived in the area came to visit. Even the local French government administrator came. Everyone realized that if the fever did not break, the child would die.

"We certainly regret that your daughter is ill, Monsieur and Madame Metzler. Is there anything we can do to help?"

"No, thank you," they answered. "But you're very kind. You see, we gave our little Lilianne over to our Lord's hands. He gave her to us in the first place, and now if He wants her back it's up to Him. We know she accepted Jesus as her Savior, so we'll see her again in Heaven where there's no more sickness and suffering."

The parents could even smile at the thought of such reassurance in Christ.

How odd these people are, thought the administrator. He wondered if their God really was as trustworthy and loving as they thought He was.

Lilianne's condition worsened. Paul drove home to Balimba for more clothes for her, assuming her hospital stay would be prolonged. When he returned, Lilianne opened her eyes.

"Do you know who this is?" Etiennette asked her.

The child looked over at her father and nodded, then slowly closed her eyes. She never reopened them. An hour later she went to be with the Lord.

Loving hands prepared little Lilianne for burial and dressed her. The French administrator came to express his sympathy that evening.

He gazed down at the lifeless body a moment and then, puzzled, turned to Paul.

"Do you realize she has a smile on her face? She seems to be happy."

"Yes, she is happy. She is now with her Lord."

No other missionary preacher was present to conduct the funeral, so Paul took charge the following day. Despite his sense of loss, he looked forward to the opportunity to preach to the Europeans who would come. For years the missionaries had tried unsuccessfully to reach them. Shortly, white faces joined the hundreds of Africans who encircled the cemetery.

Paul began. "Even a child can understand how God sent His Son Jesus Christ to save us. He paid the penalty for our sins because we can't do it ourselves and still live. Lilianne accepted the gift of forgiveness of sins and asked Christ to be her Lord and Savior, and now she is living in Heaven with Him."

Paul knew many in the audience were hearing the gospel for the first time.

"Do you mind if I say a few words?" requested the government administrator when the message ended.

Paul stepped down a bit reluctantly, remembering a funeral he had preached for a European child a few weeks ago. That day he had warned that only in Christ was anyone free from the horrors of Hell. Then the administrator had accused God of injustice for having taken such a young life. What would he say this time?

"Lilianne," he addressed himself to the lifeless little body, "yesterday I went to the hospital to offer consolation to your parents, but instead they consoled me. I went there not believing in God or Heaven or Hell. Now, Lilianne, I believe there is a Heaven and I believe you are there."

Paul wiped a tear from his eye. This man's heart had been so hard, but the Lord had reached him through a little girl.

The mourners lined up to offer their sympathy to the parents. One Frenchman broke rank and slipped away without so much as a nod. What could be wrong? Metzlers had been friends a long time with Monsieur Tiran, and he had taken time to visit Lilianne in the hospital. The line pressed closer, demanding attention. Paul and Etiennette had to settle for a quick prayer for their friend.

The parents determined to turn their attention now to their work and their other children.

Fearless Ralph had to be watched every minute. One day he asked his mother for a big stick. She sent him to Saria, the houseboy who idolized him and always stood ready to cater to his every whim.

No thump, no bang, no crack, no noise at all. What could the child be doing? Etiennette went to investigate and found Ralph standing on his bed trying to knock down a four-foot boa constrictor that had wrapped itself around one of the bamboo rafters in the roof. She gasped. Then she grabbed the boy and the stick and fled. It may have been a baby boa, but it was plenty big enough for a seven-year-old to leave alone. Etiennette had just lost one child, but this one was safe, praise the Lord.

CHAPTER
16

**An accident breaks Paul's back.
The new baby dies.**

Etiennette watered the flowers in front of her house one evening in late fall of 1938. A little African boy came around the corner of the house and stood watching her.

"Madame," he said nonchalantly, "your car hurt Monsieur a lot."

Etiennette studied the boy. Was he serious? If so, why was he so calm about it?

Suddenly someone shouted in alarm. Etiennette's head jerked up and she dropped her sprinkling can. She sprang into step with the missionaries and Africans racing toward the garage.

Inside she could see several workmen straining to lift the back end of the sedan and the Rev. Einfeldt crouching beside the back wheel. Where was Paul? The last she had seen him, he had headed out of the house saying he had to check the oil level of the rear differential. She did not know what that meant, but she did know he had wanted to get the car ready for the thousand miles of lonely roads to Bangassou.

Etiennette found one of the men she knew had been helping Paul.

"Well, he decided to change the brake bands," he explained, craning his neck to watch the rescue efforts. "We used that block and tackle to lift the rear end onto blocks so we could reach the brakes. We had almost finished when Monsieur went into the house for a drink of water, and we finished changing the bands."

He stooped to see what was going on under the car, and stiffened. He straightened slowly and swallowed with difficulty.

"The support blocks," he said quietly. "They are gone. Someone must have put them away when we straightened up our mess."

"Is that important?"

"Well, that means that only the block and tackle held the rear end up. Whatever Monsieur did must have put enough pressure on the rope to snap it."

By now the car had been moved away from Paul, but he still lay unconscious on the dusty floor. Etiennette found a rag and tried to wipe off the worst of the foul-smelling oil from his face and hands. One of the missionaries came over to help.

"It looks like he was sitting underneath the car," he said. "See that wrench and the can of hypoid oil? Apparently he had trouble loosening the plug to check the oil. It looks like the car fell on his shoulders."

Paul groaned, his eyes slowly opening. A few men rushed over to help him up, but he groaned again.

"Don't touch me," he managed to get out. "Bring a plank."

Etiennette flew into the house for some pills. Just the few words he spoke and the effort of taking the painkillers exhausted the victim.

Sweat beads popped out on his forehead as he eased onto the plank. He squeezed his eyes shut and took a few deep breaths to conquer the nausea caused by the pain. Then he motioned for the men to carry him into the house.

"The doctor will not come, Madame," the messenger reported when he returned later that night from Fort Archambault. "He says there is nothing he can do. He is afraid there is no hope for Monsieur."

The Christians did not give up so easily. They prayed for healing and also for wisdom to know how to help. The next day they sent for Mary Kneeland, the missionary nurse from Fort Crampel, to come manage the sickroom. In the meantime Etiennette took a bamboo rug and made a corset to support her husband's back.

Paul had to stay in bed for several weeks. Christians continued to pray for him, and the Lord intervened. Finally he could pick up some of his activities, but even innocent little bumps or twists aggravated his injury. Sometimes the pain became so intense he would have to lie flat in bed for days.

"Lord," he cried out in frustration, "there are too many things to do for me to just lie here. Some villages still haven't heard the gospel and others need to hear it again. What about Bible studies and services? What about these who spend time helping me when so much needs to be done?"

A Bible verse crowded out these and other thoughts: "My grace is sufficient for thee: for my strength is made perfect in weakness" (2 Cor. 12:9).

Paul relaxed and smiled.

"Well, Lord, I did ask You to show Your strength through me when I came into missions," he said. "The rest of that verse says I need to 'glory in my infirmities, that the power of Christ may rest upon me.' I sure do need Your power, so please help me be able to glory in this pain."

"Paul, maybe you should go see a doctor in France," Etiennette urged. "Certainly there is something that could be done."

"Well, there is a lot of pain," he admitted, "but there's too much that needs to be done here. Besides, the Lord used my floating kidney to get young missionaries interested in a work at Koumra, so He probably has something just as exciting planned for this injury. We'll just keep praying."

Paul kept going with the help of the corset and the Lord.

In the last part of 1939 Etiennette gave birth to their ninth and last child. Etienne Paul was a healthy, happy baby for four and a half months. Then he came down with a terrible case of whooping cough, and picked up dysentery just as he started to recover.

"I had hoped Etienne would get well before I left," Mary Kneeland, the missionary nurse, said to Etiennette while packing. "The poor little fellow will need much care, but if Hélène and I don't get going we'll miss the bus. We'll sure be praying for you and little Etienne."

"I sure hate to leave you right now," Paul apologized to Etiennette.

"Now, no need to worry about me," she assured him. "I have taken care of a sick baby before. Besides, there are helpers here and a doctor in town, and the Lord will take care of us. Mary needs her furlough and Hélène needs to get back to school and someone has to take them, so go on now."

Etiennette did not feel so brave when they pulled out. She slowly walked back in the house to check on the baby, knowing the house-boys would keep an eye on the other children for her.

A few days later Etiennette called for a push and hurried the baby to the hospital in Fort Archambault. She had tried everything she knew, but little Etienne just kept getting worse.

"But Madame," both military doctors protested, "he looks well enough now. Go on home and let him rest. He will feel better by tomorrow."

"But his fever just broke," Etiennette protested, "and I just changed his diaper, so you cannot tell about the dysentery right now. Why not keep him overnight and watch him?"

The doctors could not be convinced, so Etiennette had to take the baby home. The dysentery took anything she tried to feed him, and the fever made him too uncomfortable to sleep well. After several days she finally sent word to the hospital that she and the baby were on their way again.

"Madame, your baby is really not very sick," the doctors insisted, "but if it makes you feel any better we will have a room on the second floor cleared out for you. That is the best we can do."

They stalked off and a French woman came over.

"Bonjour, Madame. I am the new midwife here," she said. "Our doctors are very good, but they are not used to treating babies. Please feel free to send for me if you need me."

"Merci, I will."

Etiennette had barely settled in the little room when Etienne went into convulsions.

"Quick! Get the doctor and midwife!" she cried out to the attendant.

By the time they rushed in from other parts of the hospital, the convulsions had ended.

"Ah, Madame, your baby is resting so peacefully," they crooned. "When he has these spells you talk about, you are welcome to give him cough syrup or some camphorated oil."

"Cough syrup!" the frustrated mother retorted. "My little Etienne is not coughing, I will have you know. You people are never around when he is sick so you will not believe his problem is intestinal. Why do you refuse to do any tests to determine the problem?"

"Madame, we are very busy. We cannot do everything each worried mother demands. Let us know if he gets worse," and they left the room.

Etienne slept a little and Etiennette finally was able to rest a little. Then, a few hours later, the baby had another seizure. The mother called for the attendant.

"I need to give my baby a bath to bring down his fever," she quickly explained. "Please get the water right away."

She breathed a prayer that he would hurry. She knew he had to run out to the well for pitchers of cold water, and then get hot water from the outside kitchen.

She took down a blanket and wrapped up Etienne. The attendant ought to have everything ready by now. The baby stiffened into another seizure, so she held him carefully as she hurried across the windy veranda. Why did the bathroom have to be so far away? She sped down the stairway and then back along another long veranda.

The baby relaxed by the time they reached the bathroom, but his mother sponged him off anyway. She clutched him close as she took him back upstairs.

"This one too, Lord?"

She hesitated, then whispered, "Yes, Lord, he is Yours. Thank You for being here."

She could practically feel the life go out of her son. She hugged him, then laid him back down in his bed.

"Could you please tell the doctor and the midwife I need to see them when they have time," she asked the attendant.

No need to hurry them now.

"Look how distended his little abdomen is," said the younger doctor. "I wonder if this little fellow really did have an intestinal disease."

Why would it matter now, Etiennette wondered as she sat watching the attendants clean and dress the little body. When did we lose Marcel? She tried to remember. Thirteen years ago or so. Then there was Lilianne last year. Six years old. She felt helpless. Why do You ask so much of Your missionaries, Lord?

Then another thought crowded into her foggy mind. If it hurt so much to lose her children, how must God the Father have felt when His only Son Jesus died at Calvary? No wonder the sky grew so dark that day. Oh, God could not look at the sin His Son bore, but that darkness must have also reflected His terrible grief. Etiennette clung to the God Who understood her emptiness.

Now, who would preach the funeral message? Paul was still gone, and there were no other men at the station in Balimba at the time. Mr. Burkhardt and Mr. Rogers from the Brethren mission took over for her, giving a clear testimony to the Africans and Europeans who attended.

"Madame, we have never heard anything quite like that before," the doctors and midwife told Etiennette afterward. "We will have to think about it."

Etiennette's spirits lifted. God can certainly use the most awful circumstances to bring glory to Himself, she thought. The words to a song popped into her mind.

Sometimes the clouds of trouble
Bedim the sky above,
I cannot see my Savior's face,
I doubt His wondrous love;
But He, from Heaven's mercy seat,
Beholding my despair,
In pity bursts the clouds between
And shows me He is there.

It's just like Jesus to roll the clouds away,
It's just like Jesus to keep me day by day,
It's just like Jesus all along the way—
It's just like His great love!

* * *

Paul, Hélène and Mary Kneeland bounced along on their way to Fort Lamy (now N'Djamene), the capital of Chad, praying for baby Etienne's recovery. They knew they would have to wait until they arrived to get any news.

"What's that you're doing over there, Hélène?" her father asked.

"Taking notes," she answered, lifting her pencil off the page while the car shuddered from the bumpy road. "I'll rewrite them into a journal in the evenings, and send back a copy. It'll be almost as if you went with me all the way to America this time, Papa."

"Just like a newspaper reporter, huh?" he smiled.

"Well, I do like to write," she smiled back shyly.

"I think you'd have a wonderful perspective, Hélène," Mary put in. "Everything's especially adventurous to a fifteen-year-old. Why don't you read us your latest entry each morning?"

CHAPTER
17

**The oldest daughter goes
to Amercia to school.**

My Trip to America, through the Sahara, in 1940
by Hélène Metzler

"Miss Kneeland, Father and I left Fort Archambault the 23rd of March, at about 4:30 P.M. We drove until 2:15 A.M. the next day, and then stopped at a rest house. Father made a bed in the car out of the seat, and Miss Kneeland and I slept in the house on our cots. We slept very well, and by 8:00 the next morning we were on our way again with a good breakfast in our stomachs and a good night's rest.

"Since it was Sunday, and especially Easter Sunday, we expected to drive only a little that morning and stay someplace along the way until sometime in the late afternoon, and then start out again. We drove until about 10:00 A.M. and started hunting for a rest house. We drove and drove, but couldn't find any. The country through which we were driving was very dry, and the trees were almost bare. The villages were about twenty miles apart because there was not much water near. We were as hot and sleepy as could be, and we could not find a rest house or even a big shade tree under which to rest. We drove until 2:00 P.M. and then—a rest house. Even though it had been used for goats and perhaps cows and had quite a lot of dirt in it, it was as welcome as a mansion to us. We had our dinner, and Father slept a bit. At 3:30 P.M. we started on. We were hoping to arrive at Fort Lamy that night, but when we were a few kilometers from the river, the car stopped short to let us know that its tank was empty and it would not go on thirsty. (There was a big sandbank just before the river, and on the other side of the river is Fort Lamy.)

"Father got out, and what do you suppose he did? The two African men who were with us had brought along a small bottle of kerosene for the lanterns, and he poured that in, and the car was satisfied for about three kilometers (nearly two miles). Then Father emptied the kerosene from the lanterns into the tank, and we were off again. At last we came to the place where the road turns off toward the river, and what a road! It was piled up with sand and rotten wood, and on one side all we could see was sand until the river. And that was a wide stretch too. The good old car started puffing, and she puffed and she puffed and she puffed, and then she got tired and decided that she would go no farther. We all got out and pushed and pushed, but she had made up her mind and she was not willing to change it.

"We had Mamadou from Fort Crampel with us and also our kitchen helper, so Father sent Mamadou to ask Mr. Olley, the missionary at Fort Lamy, for some gas. We waited and waited until about 6:30, and then we started getting supper ready. We ate and rolled up in blankets on the sand. It was cold. Soon we heard mosquitoes buzzing hungrily about us, so we put the net over our small folding table and put our heads underneath. After we'd been lying there a while, Mamadou came with the gas and said that the ferry would not take us across at night, so we slept there in the moonlight all night, wrapped up in our blankets.

"Every time I awakened, I could see all around me nearly as plainly as in the daytime, and I could see the lights of Fort Lamy twinkling across the river.

"At 4:00 this morning, we got up and it was so cold we had to wear our coats. We got across the ferry after much pushing, and we arrived here about 8:30 A.M.

"Since it is a holiday here today, we cannot buy in any store and so we are having a good day of rest. We saw many antelopes, monkeys and guinea fowls on our way here, and we ran over one small antelope and killed it. We also killed two guinea fowls and saw two pigs, and that's all about animals for today. I will write a little more tonight, to tell about the rest of the day.

"11:00 P.M. I am writing this in bed by the light of a lantern while Miss Kneeland is getting ready for bed. We went through the market today, and the ways here are very different from Fort Archambault. The women have quite long hair in small braids, hanging down their necks. Most of the people here are Arabs, but there are some who belong to different tribes, who have come to visit or trade. We went to a meeting this evening where Mr. Olley showed lantern slides of creation.

"March 26th. We went to many different places today, to get papers signed, etc., and we also saw many animals. The bus has not arrived yet today, and we're hoping it will arrive soon. A man in town said that many buses leave late, but we are hoping this one won't, for we just found out that it takes eighteen days, instead of fourteen, to Algiers now. They said that Miss Kneeland and I will be the only women passengers as far as Kano, where we should arrive after two days. Then at Kano, they do not know if there will be any women passengers.

"March 27th. We've certainly had a nice time today. Every day seems more interesting than the one before. We had our baggage weighed, and it was just a little over the amount allowed each passenger, so we won't have to pay much extra. We also found out that we have to take our own food, water, cots and bedding; and we were surprised, for we did not expect to have to take so much. The bus has not arrived yet, so this means that we won't go tomorrow. We certainly hope it comes tomorrow. This morning we went for a ride in the 'wilds' and stopped on the road to have some tea. We killed a rabbit also. Mr. Olley is enjoying our visit very much. He is the one who suggested this ride, and he often takes us to see different things around here. He has quite a sense of humor, and he is always telling jokes. He does a great deal of work for one person. He gives out medicine, has reading classes, and so many other things that I cannot write them all down.

"When we returned from our ride, we saw an Arabian wedding. The people were taking the bride to the bridegroom's house. They were all loaded with things that they were going to eat, and many of them had a large pile of presents on their heads. They were singing and dancing and beating drums and another kind of instrument that resembles a cymbal. We looked for the bride, but we couldn't see her.

"March 28th. We're still here. The bus has not arrived, and the man who is in charge says it will perhaps arrive tomorrow. We hope it's true.

"We saw the same wedding procession go by today again. Mr. Olley says that they sometimes keep it up for a whole week. We did not go anywhere today; we just rested and did different things in the house. We see lots of camels every day, for they carry things here to trade and sell for their masters.

"Miss Kneeland felt quite tired today, and this evening at about 5:00 she got a fever. She went to bed without any supper and she had chills for a while, but she will be all right tomorrow morning. We hope so.

"March 29th. Still here. The bus has not arrived yet. We are going to go and see what the man knows about it tomorrow morning. Miss Kneeland has been in bed all day. She is not very sick, but does not feel well enough to get up.

"Every day, from morning 'till quite a while after dark, we hear little boys from seven to ten years old yelling very loudly, 'Milk to sell, milk to sell.' Their fathers raise cows and sell the milk to other Africans, so they send their children out to sell it for them. They also sell camel's milk.

"March 30th. This afternoon, at about 5:30, we received very sad news, telling us that our dear little Etienne went to the 'Home for little children, up above the bright blue sky.' We were very sad to hear it, but could say only 'Have Thine own way, Lord.'

"This morning we went to see the man in charge of this bus business, and he said he knew nothing about it; but his clerk, who is an African who speaks English, said it should arrive sometime today and that we would leave Monday at seven in the morning, if so. Here's hoping it's true.

"March 31st. Well, it was no use hoping, for the bus has not arrived.

153

The man in charge doesn't seem to care what happens. Every time we ask him, he shrugs his shoulders and says that he knows nothing about it. Perhaps it will come tomorrow. We hope it will come soon, or we shall miss our boat to Marseilles [France].

"Today is Sunday, but Mr. Olley's meetings are usually so long, he told us that we didn't have to go; so we went only for communion. (He has to have his sermon translated into many different languages.)

"April 1st. This is April Fool's Day, but we have not played any tricks. The bus hasn't come either. Father went home this morning at 11:00 and left us 'on our own.' We are finding out about the aeroplane, and if we can get reservations for Friday's plane, and if the bus has not arrived by then, we'll go by plane. We hope the bus will arrive by that time, though, because we would rather go on it, for many reasons."

* * *

Paul had felt he really needed to get back to his wife. The news about Etienne had arrived two days earlier, so even the funeral would be over by now. He hated to leave Mary with all the responsibility when she still had not fully recovered from her fever, but the bus could not possibly delay much longer. Besides, Mr. Olley would be certain to help out. Paul hurried home.

The bus did finally come on April 4 and left on the 5th. They crossed the Sahara Desert going north to Algeria, and then on to France before reaching America.

CHAPTER
18

**World War II frightens foreigners,
Paul acts as a liaison with officials,
the family sails home
despite the German navy.**

What do you hear from the BBC [British Broadcasting Corporation]?" a missionary from Kyabe asked.

"The Axis Powers seem to be swallowing whole countries," George Sinderson replied, frowning.

He and his wife had come from Koumra to join the other missionaries gathering at Fort Archambault to follow the progress of the war. The station ministries continued, but special prayer groups met every day.

"What do you think will happen to the African colonies if France surrenders to Germany?" one missionary asked.

The others sitting around the radio shifted nervously in their chairs.

"What about Italy?" another spoke up. "It's directly north of here. Do you think Mussolini would be bold enough to create a provisional government on African soil? He did take Ethiopia in '35."

"And don't forget that England has declared war now too," George said. "Ella and I are British subjects, you know. If the Axis Powers do take over Africa, what will they do to us? Bessie [Falle] and Florence [Stacey] are subjects too."

He frowned, then added, "I wonder if we should just leave the country until this is over."

"Even if we all left, our national brethren will still be here," another missionary reminded them. "Fascists don't seem to like any color Christian."

"Well, I for one will help Chad if it comes to that," Paul said. "Back in '39 when France first declared war on Germany, I telegraphed the Governor General that I'd be willing to help in some civil service. Maybe they'll need to treat wounded men here at the dispensary or something. He said he'd keep in touch."

The Axis Powers kept advancing on all fronts. The BBC reported the destruction and oppression, and the missionaries' worst fears became more and more realistic.

"We had better send a representative to Brazzaville to keep closer tabs on things than we can do here," a missionary suggested one evening. "We need someone to let us know how we should respond."

The others agreed and chose Paul to go, since he was president of the Chad and Central African Field Council.

"Well, I checked the car and trailer over," he reported to the others the next day. "They're ready to go now. Had to clean out the carburetor after the trip to Fort Lamy with Hélène and Mary. Guess we'll be all set in a week or so."

That evening the BBC announced that the German army had sneaked around the French army's "impregnable" Maginot line of defense. They would reach Paris the next day. Etiennette had to sit down.

Paul broke the stunned silence.

"We'll leave tomorrow morning," he muttered.

The good-byes were strained. No one knew when they would see each other again. Even Saria, the houseboy, mourned for his favorite charge.

"Madame," he wailed to Etiennette, "who will make my Ralph's bed in America?"

Paul and Etiennette stopped by the "missionary kids' school" at Fort Sibut for their three older children. Thirteen-year-old Rachel and eleven-year-old Edwin knew that they might end up in a concentration camp if French Equatorial Africa sided with the Vichy French as rumored. A Frenchwoman married to an American would not be safe from these traitors, nor would her family because the United States backed the English against the Nazis.

Nine-year-old Ralph understood that his teachers and parents and even his older sister and brother seemed extra sober lately. Well, they could worry about whatever it was. He intended to enjoy this vacation from school. Besides, five-year-old Jack and three-year-old Evelyne looked to him for fun.

The next day the family reached Bangui and boarded the riverboat to Brazzaville, the capital of French Equatorial Africa. Even the older children could not resist the excitement and joined the others at the railing.

"There's another croc," Ralph called out. "See him? He's trying to get a suntan."

Jack ran to see.

"That's no crocodile," Edwin snorted. "It's just part of the sandbar."

"Yes, it is," Ralph shot back. "See? It moved its tail a little."

"A hippo!" Rachel waved to the others. "Come look! He's playing with his brother."

Evelyne ran over and climbed up on some boxes in order to see. She laughed and clapped her hands. The children played on deck as much as possible that week, keeping an eye out for any new creature to entertain them.

As the capital came into sight, a speedboat roared out toward them.

"France has surrendered!" one man shouted. "Stay away from Brazzaville!"

The riverboat captain barked an order, and his vessel turned sharply toward the Belgian Congo shore. In Leopoldville (now

Kinshasa) Paul arranged several meetings with the American and British counsuls.

"You know, Rev. Metzler," they finally advised him, "you could do more for the other missionaries if you were in the United States. Besides," one lowered his voice, "just between us, in a few days Chad will join the Allies. This will assure the safety of any missionaries who stay behind in both the Chad and the Oubangui Chari [now the Central African Republic]."

"Well, that's a relief," Paul said gratefully. "I sure hate to leave, though. I'd rather stay and help."

He paused to think, then looked back up.

"But if you really think I can help by going to America, I will."

"Good," the consul nodded, then added, "but remember, passenger ships don't dare push off from the West Coast these days. Try Cape Town. It's safer."

"But Cape Town is at least 4,500 miles away," Etiennette protested to Paul later.

"Well," he shrugged, "I guess we'll get to see the southern part of the continent this trip."

The American consul sent for Paul the following week.

"I'll be strapping the last box of canned goods down in a few days," Paul reported to the consul, sinking gratefully into a chair. "Then we're ready to go south."

"Well," the consul paused, grinning already at the expected response. "Would you by chance be interested in sailing directly from Matadi?"

"Of course," the missionary said, jumping up. "I'd be thrilled to save a few thousand miles and drive just to the mouth of the Congo River. Praise God!"

"Now, you're still running a risk sailing with German U-boats in the Atlantic," the consul went on. "If you're going to go, you'll have to sign a paper that you have been warned. Still interested?"

"Yes, the Lord will protect us."

"Then make reservations as soon as possible for the *S.S. Leopoldville*. She's sailing nonstop to New York."

He sighed and shook his head sadly.

"She's the last of the once proud Belgian fleet."

Two other missionary families arrived in nearby Leopoldville while Paul was selling the car and trailer and accumulated supplies. Fogles and Teachouts bought their tickets and signed the necessary releases, then joined Metzlers on the train to Matadi.

"I am sorry, but all passengers on the *Leopoldville* must travel first

159

class," the clerk who checked their tickets informed them. "Let me see that will be another—"

"But we can't possibly afford to pay the first-class fare," Paul interrupted. "Who may we talk to to straighten this out?"

"Well, all right, we will let you go for the second-class fare," the authorities finally agreed, "but you must use the first-class accommodations. The other passengers are a Belgian couple who have paid for first class services, and we see no reason to open a second dining room or another deck of rooms just for you."

The missionaries thanked the Lord for such a wonderful treat. The children had plenty of room to play on this four-hundred passenger ocean liner, and the parents could enjoy its luxuries.

Two days out of port the ship turned completely around and headed back.

"Captain, what's the matter?" the alarmed missionaries asked.

"This cable came this morning. My orders are to return to Matadi. Something must have happened."

The missionaries held a prayer meeting. In less than an hour the ship again reversed directions and headed back out to sea.

"I received another telegram," the captain smiled at his guests. "Apparently the first one was not sent by the Belgian government at all. It probably came from one of the German subs or the raiders we know are in these waters. We will acknowledge no other orders."

"The Germans will just have to get God's permission to bother us," piped up one of the children.

The others giggled and ran off to play.

Despite this triumph, signs of danger loomed about the ship. Who could help but notice that all the lifeboats hung partway down the ship's sides, ready to be lowered at a moment's notice if the ship were hit by a torpedo. Would a lifeboat take them to the New York harbor?

To avoid detection, no lights were allowed after dark. God provided the moon and the stars, though, so the missionaries gathered on deck every evening to sing hymns.

"Whatsamatter with you people, anyway?" a crewman taunted. "Don't you know there's a war on? This ship could go down at any time, an' there you sit like you're enjoyin' yourselves. This ain't no Sunday School picnic, y'know."

"But you see," answered Paul, "if this ship goes down, we'll go up."

This conviction upheld the missionary families throughout the uncertain voyage. The children quickly forgot the danger as they romped on deck, the braver boys even climbing the rigging.

For days the ship inched along, propellers barely moving. Frustrated, Paul once again approached the captain for an explanation.

"Well, Monsieur," came the reply, "see how tall our smokestack is? Just imagine smoke billowing out of it as we sped along. Now, can you imagine how easily those U-boats could see us? We would be waving a red flag in front of a bull. Besides, we need to conserve our fuel oil in order to make the trip as far as New York."

One night a few days later, however, the ship lurched forward, waking all its passengers. The engines churned at full speed ahead. Early the next morning Paul and Etiennette found the captain on deck.

"Why did you change your mind about the speed?"

"We intercepted an SOS from a British vessel off the coast of Florida. They are under attack by *Graf Spee,* the German raider, and they are sinking. Guess we will not follow the American coastline after all."

If hostile powers were ignoring the neutrality of an uncommitted country, were any waters really safe? Now the *S. S. Leopoldville* puffed along at high speed toward New York more concerned with avoiding the *Graf Spee* than with being seen.

Then one morning the sailors hoisted up the lifeboats and returned them to storage. Laughter erupted from knots of sailors attending leisurely to their duties. Not even a holiday would have caused such a change. What could possibly have happened?

"Oh, we have passed the Norfolk naval bases on the Virginia coast," explained the captain. "Even the *Graf Spee* would not dare pursue us past the American fleet."

Now the passengers really felt safe. The next day New York harbor loomed into view. As the ship gratefully anchored in protected waters, Rachel and Edwin raced to find their parents.

"Mother! Father! Come quick!"

"What on earth is the matter?" Etiennette demanded as she and Paul appeared around one corner. "We are busy gathering up all our things to go ashore. What can be so exciting?"

"A circus is coming on board!" Edwin panted out.

"Complete with clowns!" confirmed Rachel. "Come on!"

The other children rushed to see, but when the parents saw the "circus," they laughed the loudest.

"That's no circus," Paul said, still chuckling. "Those are American news reporters with press hats on."

"They probably want to question the captain about German interference during our trip," another adult added, smiling at the deflated youngsters.

"Come now, and let us get ready to go ashore," Etiennette urged.

CHAPTER
19

The Lord provides finances and clothing after the hasty trip to the States.
Time together, then school for the
older children. The two youngest
accompany their folks on the dangerous trip back to Africa.
America is now in the war.

The missionaries passed through customs in New York City after the banks closed on Saturday. They counted a total of $12 among all three families. At least it would pay their taxi fare to the National Bible Institute.

Metzlers' children gawked out the windows all the way through the city. No other place they could remember looked quite like this.

"Look at all that wasted cement!" Edwin finally burst out.

Although the adults laughed, they had to agree.

The Institute gladly provided accommodations for the families over the weekend until they could get funds from the Mission.

Monday morning they received a letter from the home office asking them all to come over to Paterson, New Jersey, for a missionary conference. Etiennette eyed the khaki shorts and sleeveless pullovers her boys had on. They looked fine for Africa but not for a conference in America. Where would they find proper clothes at a price they could afford? Etiennette asked God for help, and within a few hours a local assistant pastor called.

"My wife and children are away," Tom Clark explained, "so I have plenty of room for visitors. Why don't you come on over?"

When the Metzlers arrived, Pastor Clark opened a wardrobe and insisted they use some of his boys' suits. Once again God had supplied.

While attending this conference in Paterson, Paul was asked to speak at a church back across the New York line in Ozone Park, Brooklyn. It meant crossing Manhattan and driving through many city streets. This would be a chance to practice driving his "new" car with the gearshift on the steering wheel. What an odd place for it, he mused. He set out early Sunday morning with Edwin and Ralph for moral support.

What a trip! There were traffic lights overhead, to the right or the left, and even where least expected—in the center of the road. In Africa there might be washouts, broken bridges, bush fires or trees across the road to contend with, but these seemed minor compared with all the lights.

"Now boys, you must watch the lights for me," instructed Paul, gripping the wheel.

The boys tried, but more than once they called out, "Father, you just went through another red light."

"Please don't wait until afterwards," their father begged. "You must tell me before we get to it."

Besides the lights, directional signs demanded attention. Paul's head spun. He did his best, but he just was not used to the car or the big city. He praised the Lord there was little traffic so early on Sunday morning and no policemen out. The three arrived at the church grateful to God for a safe, if turbulent, trip.

God blessed in the service and also provided a good offering to help buy clothes for the children.

Soon the Metzler family began their trip to Mishawaka. When they needed to stop for gas and refreshments, they usually chose a Sunoco station where a waitress would bring sandwiches to the car. After one such dinner, Edwin seemed especially pleased.

"Isn't it nice of our cousins to wait on us?" he said.

"Cousins? That was not your cousin," Etiennette corrected, puzzled. Edwin's smile melted.

"But Father said we'd meet cousins in America," he protested.

"Oh, I remember," Paul grinned, "but I didn't mean these waitresses. You'll meet your cousins before long."

When they did meet their cousins, Rachel and Ralph teased Edwin about his other "cousins."

After about a year of furlough, the Metzlers again prepared to return to the Chad. This time, however, they left four of their six children at the Westervelt Home in South Carolina for schooling. Several other missionaries from central Africa had done the same. Only six-year-old Jack and four-year-old Evelyne were to return to Africa with their parents.

The children had gone to school away from home before, but only Hélène had gone to school halfway around the world. The good-byes were tearful, but Paul and Etiennette believed this was part of God's will for their family.

Next the parents concentrated on finding transportation to Africa—no easy task with a global war in full swing. All the freighters were carrying gasoline and ammunition and refused the responsibility of couples with children. What were they going to do? God knew the shipping routes, and surely He would help them find a way to cross the sea.

Paul decided to check out an alternative when traveling the West Coast for meetings. Why not take a liner from San Francisco to the east coast of Africa? He booked passage to Nairobi before leaving for home.

Satan thought he had us, thought Paul triumphantly as he drove home, but God opened the back door.

However, the god of this world had not given up yet. He arranged a "surprise." Metzlers received a notice of cancellation a few days before shipping their baggage from Indiana. The government had requisitioned the ship along with many others. Another setback.

Paul found himself wondering if God had changed His mind about sending him and his family back to Africa. But no, He had not changed His mind. This cancellation had to fit in His will somehow. Later news came that the ship they had been booked on had been captured by the Japanese at Singapore, and all the British and French citizens had been sent to a concentration camp. That might have included Etiennette, Jack and Evelyne. Satan's attempt to outsmart God had played right into His hand.

Again Metzlers turned to God for transportation to Africa. One day they received a letter from Miss Mary Kneeland saying that she had been able to book passage for them along with her own. Instead of shipping their baggage to San Francisco, they shipped it to New York City. As soon as the family arrived in New York, Paul went to the office of the shipping company.

"Excuse me," Paul caught the clerk's attention. "What papers do I need to fill out in order to take my car and trailer with me on the boat?"

The shipping clerk's eyebrows raised nearly up to his hairline.

"Your car and trailer? Didn't you receive our letter saying that you could not take baggage on this ship? Just your cabin luggage."

Now it was Paul's turn to be surprised.

"No, I sure didn't. In fact, more than three tons of baggage have already been shipped here for this voyage. We're taking things for many of the missionaries who have been without supplies for some time."

"I'm sorry about the misunderstanding, sir, but it's impossible for you to take the car."

"But I must have my car to make the trip inland from the coast of Africa. It's twelve hundred miles."

"I'm sorry, sir."

"We'll see."

Paul left the office praying, determined to find a way.

As the missionaries awaited departure, their baggage began arriving. At the last minute they bought two more trunks and filled them with bandages, medicines, food and clothing. No sooner had the last trunk been delivered than word came to board ship the next day at 11:00 A.M.

"Etiennette," Paul instructed on boarding day, "you hire a taxi and take the children to the boat. I'm going to get the necessary papers for shipping the car."

Once again he strode into the shipping office and asked for the forms to ship his car. The clerk raised his voice loud enough for everyone in the office to hear his reply.

"I've already told you three or four times that it's impossible to take

167

that car on this liner," he shouted.

Paul took a deep breath to retort, but before he could do so the clerk leaned toward him confidentially.

"Go down and drive your car on the dock," he whispered, and handed Paul a pass.

The Lord had solved that nicely, but there still remained another "impossible" job to be done. Paul had a pocketful of checks from many different churches and individuals to pay the passage to Africa. Now, how would he get these cashed in just two hours before the ship sailed? The banks in New York refused to cash checks for anyone passing through because of the war, and of course checks were no good in Africa.

Standing right there in front of the dock, Paul prayed. "Lord, what is my next move?"

The name of a fellow missionary came to mind.

"Oh yes, Lord, I remember. Mrs. Braun has a brother who owns a business here. Maybe he will know what to do. Thank You, Lord."

Paul quickly found his name in the phone book and gave him a call.

"Of course I can help. Come on down to my office and I'll call my bank. All I have to do is initial your checks and you'll get the money. They'll use my business as collateral. No problem."

With only a few minutes to spare, Paul reached the ship with cash in hand to pay their way. God always pays for His business, thought Paul. He definitely wants us aboard the *Arcadia*.

As the ship pulled out of the harbor that night, Mary Kneeland and the Metzler family gathered at the bow and sang "Safe Am I." They knew this trip back to Africa would certainly be more dangerous than when they had gone on furlough just a year ago, but they knew God would take care of them.

Some of the young men on deck leaned on the rails within earshot to listen. Others just shook their heads at these "fanatics" who did not seem to understand reality as they did. Maybe the twenty-eight assorted missionaries on board thought this was just another cruise, but the young men knew that danger lurked as close as a German submarine or a reconnaissance flight, especially if their civilian disguises did not hold up. As members of United States Army engineering crews, they were on a secret mission to lay airstrips across Africa.

Besides the danger of the trip itself, the passengers' faith in their ship took a beating. They learned that she had formerly traveled only along the coast between New York and Boston, and this was her first trans-Atlantic voyage. The missionaries praised God they could trust Him anyway.

As they made their way down the coast to Belém, Brazil, they traveled in a blackout. Passengers were warned not even to smoke on deck after dark. When they arrived at Belém, the crew of the ship went on strike, refusing to go farther without an escort.

Maybe we should have listened to the warnings after all, mused Paul. Several Christians said we are foolish to travel during the war, especially with children. It's true that boats are sunk every day.

Paul straightened his shoulders.

"No, Lord," he said aloud. "We did the right thing to come. You are leading us. What is there to fear?"

The *Arcadia* finally left port, escorted by a cruiser and two destroyers. Despite this added security, the soldiers took their mattresses to the top deck every night to sleep.

"Mr. Metzler," one of the officers asked a few days later, "why don't you missionaries sleep on the top deck? Don't you know we're in a war? This crate could be torpedoed any time. Then what would you do down there in your cabins?"

"Certainly we are aware that we're in a war, sir," came the reply, "but we trust our Lord to protect us. If the boat does go down, we know that we would go up to be with Him. Would you like to be sure of this too?"

The officer declined to talk further but did attend the Sunday services the missionaries held throughout the voyage. Many of the other soldiers came, too, and some even gathered around for the missionaries' nightly hymn sings. Of course, some of the men made fun, but most joined in. Some even requested favorite hymns they had learned when they were children. The missionaries thanked God for this encouragement.

CHAPTER
20

The Lord provides transportation inland and legal entry despite gas rationing and hostile military officials. A new ministry develops to French and English soldiers training in Chad.

To maintain security, no one had been told their exact destination. When land finally did come within sight, everyone tried to guess which African port it was.

"I think it's Nigeria," one missionary ventured. "We were told to secure a visa from the British consul before leaving New York. We'd need such a visa in Nigeria."

It was, in fact, Lagos, Nigeria. The missionaries immediately went to buy gasoline for the inland trip.

"It is impossible!" the man in charge of rationing told Paul. "There is hardly enough gas to go around as it is, and you ask for enough for a long trip. Huh! Send the car by rail to Jos and get your gas there."

"That would take most of our money, and we wouldn't have enough left to finish our trip. You must give us the necessary ration tickets."

The man still refused, so Paul sighed and tried again.

"When we went to get our British visas, I told the British consul we would need gas for the inland trip. He assured me that there was no reason why we could not get gas. In fact, he said, 'All the gas they have comes from America, and you are an American citizen.' So please give me the tickets."

When all arguments failed, Paul sought out the American consul.

"You are very fortunate, Rev. Metzler," he said. "The one man in this country who can give you authorization to buy gas is in town today. Return at two o'clock this afternoon."

That afternoon the consul told Paul to go back to the ration office. This time, instead of arguing, the man politely asked Paul how much gas he needed. Paul breathed a thank-you to God. They checked the map for distance, and then the gasoline official asked about the car's gas mileage. He was determined to give only enough fuel to reach the border of Nigeria. That was all he had to do, but the border was still about one hundred and fifty miles from Fort Lamy, the nearest place where the missionaries could buy more gas.

Paul gave the correct gas mileage and prayed for a miracle to get them inland. The official carefully figured how much gas it would take in British Imperial gallons and handed over the tickets. On his way out the door, Paul suddenly realized he had just witnessed his miracle. Each Imperial gallon held five American quarts. That was an extra quart for every gallon. Paul stopped and stared at the tickets in his hand. They would get him enough gas, not only to get to the border but on to Fort Lamy and—he squeezed the tickets in a fist—all the way to Fort Archambault! The Lord had done it again.

While Paul busied himself with the gas project, Etiennette took the

173

time to dash off a letter to the children back in the States. She had already written the name of their ship and its departure date, so now she reported in prearranged codes that they had all arrived safely in Africa. She knew it would be several months before any reply came. Mail had been traveling slower than snails since the war began. Sometimes letters never did arrive if they had been intercepted and sounded suspicious. She breathed a prayer that the codes would keep the letter safe and that it would reach the children.

Now that Paul had arranged personal transportation inland, attention turned to the baggage. It could ride the train as far as Jos, Nigeria, along with Mary Kneeland, Etiennette and the children. Paul drove to Jos, praying earnestly for a way to get all that baggage to Balimba.

While he endured the several days' trip alone, the women and children settled in on the train.

"Now Jack and Evelyne," they instructed, "you must sleep on top of the sheets. All sorts of people have slept in these bunk beds, and germs are undoubtedly all over this compartment."

The children nodded gravely. This was another wartime restriction.

"Help! Help! Mother!"

Screams pierced the night. Etiennette jumped out of bed while Mary flipped on the light. Evelyne sat trembling on her bare bunk with the sheet twisted around her feet.

"Mother," she sobbed, "the Germans are all over me!"

It took Etiennette some time to realize the frightened little girl had just confused "germs" with "Germans." The rest of the trip proved anticlimactic.

"Monsieur Metzler," an Arabian merchant approached Paul as soon as he arrived in Jos, "I would count it a privilege to take your baggage to Fort Lamy by truck."

God had prepared the solution to the transportation problem while the missionaries traveled.

"It is the end of the rainy season you know, Monsieur and Madame Metzler," an official in Jos warned. "The roads are probably not open yet. You know how slippery this black gumbo dirt is when it gets wet. Unless the sun shines brighter than usual, you will never be able to drive to Fort Lamy, especially pulling a loaded trailer."

Again, the family and Mary asked God to intervene. The next morning the sun came out in full force. Perspiration beaded on their foreheads and trickled down their backs. God answers prayer wholeheartedly, mused Paul.

The next afternoon the missionaries began their journey with well over one-hundred-degree temperatures. A nice tall glass of ice cold Coca-Cola would sure taste good now, Paul thought as he drove along. He glanced over to see who was still awake.

"Mary," he said over engine and road noise, "do you know what I'm thinking about?"

"Sure, I'm thinking about the same thing."

"Do you remember how we griped about paying fifteen cents for one of those glasses on board ship?"

"I sure do," she smiled, "but I'd pay fifty cents or double to get one right now."

"Me too."

Then he shook his head. "But we know there are no soft drink stands on this road." He paused, then added, "But, praise the Lord, at least we're in Africa, iced drinks or not."

At last they reached Fort Lamy. In a few hours they received an urgent summons from the military commander. On his way over to the colonel's office, Paul dropped in to see the governor.

Although Governor Felix Eboué was absent, his lieutenant extended a warm welcome. He knew the governor had been friends with the missionary for years. He also remembered the letter of congratulations Paul had written when Chad became the first African colony to declare itself aligned with the Free French and General de Gaulle. The American people admired courage like that, the letter had said. Paul had promised to pray for the governor and had personally contacted many Christians who promised to pray as well. Paul had finished the letter by offering to be of service if possible when he returned to Chad, which should be soon. He wanted to help the French people regain their freedom.

"Did you receive the letter Governor Eboué sent you?" the lieutenant asked as he waved Paul to a seat. "He wanted to thank you for the prayers on his behalf. These days we all can use them."

"Yes," came the reply. "He was kind. I especially appreciated his efforts to be sure we could return to Africa."

"And that letter should help if the colonel gives you a rough time," the lieutenant smiled. "He knows no one can get a visa the usual way now that the Germans have taken control of Paris and the colonial office. He must be careful of newcomers, but if he becomes overzealous just show him the part that says, 'This letter will serve as a visa for you and your family to enter into the Chad.' "

"Well," Paul said slowly, "that's a relief. Thank you."

Paul rose to leave.

"When you get through there," the lieutenant added while shaking hands, "come back and tell me what happened."

Paul hurried on over to the commander's office.

"Who are you? What are you doing in this part of Africa? Where are you going?"

The missionary patiently answered all questions put to him.

"You are not wanted here. We already have too many foreigners. You are expected to leave the country within twenty-four hours."

Under the colonel's glare, the missionary reached in his pocket and pulled out his letter from the governor. The commander snatched it up. He trembled with fury and threw it back.

"You still must go," he snarled.

Paul returned to the governor's office to give his report.

"Forget about it," the lieutenant said with a wave of his hand. "The civil government is still in control of the country. You may proceed safely to Fort Archambault whenever you see fit."

Paul smiled in relief.

"Thank you for your kindness," he said. "I know my God is never caught off guard, but I don't always know how He will solve my problems. It seems He had this problem already solved even before I left the States."

When Mary and the Metzlers arrived at Fort Archambault, they found several hundred French refugees training there under orders from the Free French Army. These young men had fled France by whatever means they could find. Some had even braved the treacherous English Channel in small rowboats, preferring the risk of drowning to life under the Vichy French and Nazis.

These soldiers had received no news from home for many months and had no prospects of receiving any. In fact, many of their parents had no idea where they were. They were a lonesome, discouraged group of eighteen-to-twenty-year-olds, especially now during the Christmas season.

The missionaries rushed an invitation to a Christmas program over to these boy-soldiers. Two days before Christmas of 1942, the missionaries came up with another opportunity to serve Christ and France at the same time. They invited the boys to stay after the program for refreshments.

The ladies baked hundreds of cookies and several cakes to serve with coffee and lemonade, and then dug up all their sets of checkers, dominoes and chess. Paul contacted the military commander, who was delighted with this morale booster. He announced the Christmas program and food afterward at the general assembly and also posted it on the bulletin board. Almost fifty boys stayed after the program.

"We had a great time!" one of the more vocal of the group declared when they rose to go. "This would have been a terribly depressing day if you had not invited us over."

"You know," spoke up one of the younger fellows, "my mother would have made this kind of cookie at home."

He held one up for admiration.

"And my cousins and brothers always held chess tournaments during the holidays."

He looked wistfully at the game board as he spoke. After a pause he looked at the missionaries and smiled brightly.

"Thank you. It is almost like being home."

Several young heads nodded as their comrade spoke.

"Next Christmas we will spend in our beloved France!" one shouted.

It was a battle cry, drawing robust cheers from around the room.

"I have an idea," Paul put in as the exultation quieted. "How would you like to have something like this every week?"

Another round of cheers settled the matter. This was a new twist to missionary work in Chad that promised to be rewarding.

The Saturday evening meetings usually began with games, followed by a hymn sing and Bible study and, of course, ended with refreshments. Refreshments! Etiennette had never before made so many cookies and cakes, and these came during wartime rationing. The Lord miraculously provided enough ingredients to satisfy the soldiers' appetites. Etiennette often bowed over cookie dough and prayed that their spiritual appetites would eat up God's provisions in His Word.

At the first meeting Paul passed out French Sunday School hymnbooks he had just received.

"Oh, but we do not know how to sing these songs," the young men protested.

Etiennette stepped right up and said, "We will teach you."

She gladly assumed the task, and soon the soldiers knew a dozen or more hymns. The more they learned, the later the meetings lasted because they wanted to sing every song they knew before they left.

Most of these fellows came from the Department of Brittany, one of the most fanatically Roman Catholic sections of France. When Paul passed out French Gospels of John to begin a series of studies, they gasped.

"But we cannot touch these," they shrank in horror. "Our religion forbids reading or even touching the Bible."

"These are Gospels of John," Paul said.

"Oh," one breathed with relief. "We can read Gospels, just not the Bible."

News of these meetings spread to the English training camp. One day the captain in command of the Royal Air Force (RAF) at Fort Archambault approached Paul.

"Sir, would you become chaplain for my men and hold Sunday services?"

"Of course!" Paul jumped at the chance. "I'd love to share Christ with your boys too."

"We will want an Anglican service, of course," the captain went on. "We already have most of what you will need—"

"Anglican?" Paul interrupted. "But there's no place in the Anglican ritual to preach the gospel. How can I be effective if I can't even preach?"

The captain frowned thoughtfully.

"Well," he rubbed his chin a moment. "What if we make room for a gospel message each Sunday in the Anglican ceremony? Would that do?"

Paul frowned as he considered each factor carefully.

"My wife and I are Baptist by conviction," he said slowly, half to himself. "For one thing, we believe the simple way Baptists worship most closely resembles the way first-century Christians worshiped. The message is central. But Anglican ritual is so intricate it crowds out the gospel message."

He took a deep breath and let the air out slowly.

"On the other hand, these English boys are training to fight Nazis just like our French boys, and probably many will die just like our French boys. They need the gospel, too, and who else will tell them?"

After another moment of meditation, Paul agreed.

"I'll have to practice preaching in English," he grinned. "It's been French and Sango for so long."

"Rev. Metzler," several RAF trainees approached him after his first service, "the French boys come home singing every Saturday evening."

"Homemade cookies, they say, eh?" one broke in.

"I beat every bloke what lived near me at checkers," another added.

"An' they learn things, they do," the spokesman finished the appeal. "Do you 'ave a night for us?"

"Of course," Paul smiled.

Each Thursday evening for the rest of the war the RAF officers thoughtfully saved the missionaries time and gas rations by transporting their troops the three and a half miles from Fort Archambault to Balimba. More cookies and cakes came out of rationed mission kitchens, and more lemonade and coffee flowed. Best of all, God's Word flowed *unrationed* into English soldiers' hearts, and some took a definite stand for the Lord.

CHAPTER
21

Children in the States are reassured of their parents' safety, then the French troops march to D day. Family reunites during furlough; Paul has back surgery and finally finishes Bible school.

Etiennette watched the mail for news from her older four children. How had their Christmas been so far away in the United States? she wondered. Finally a letter came, fairly shouting for joy that Mother and Father and Jack and Evelyne were alive and well.

Etiennette frowned. Of course the trip to Africa had been dangerous, but why such intense reaction? Had the separation placed such a stress on the children that they had been so afraid for their parents? She read on.

The children knew from a previous letter that their parents and youngest brother and sister had sailed on the *Arcadia*. Then the radio had announced that the *Arcadia* had been sunk. Sunk! Scores died, and there were no Metzlers on the survivors' list. That could mean only one thing. The letter almost shuddered.

A few of the children left behind cried themselves to sleep every night for six weeks. The Westervelt Home and Pastor Hawkins from First Baptist Church of Mishawaka, Indiana, had begun discussing how to take care of Hélène, Rachel, Edwin and Ralph.

Mother's latest letter had finally worked its way across enemy-infested waters to say everyone was safe. They were a whole family once again. What indescribable joy!

Etiennette sat right down and wrote back that the *Arcadia* had delivered them to Nigeria ahead of schedule and had been sunk on her return voyage. God had made sure this family was safe before allowing the enemy to close in.

This same God takes care of His own on both sides of the ocean, Etiennette reminded herself. She and Paul again committed their beloved children into God's keeping so that He could clear their minds and let them pour themselves into their work.

Each Saturday night Metzlers drove into town for the meeting with the fifteen to twenty French soldiers who still came. As they studied further into the Gospel of John, the young men came up with more and more questions. They had been taught never to touch the Bible, but now they gladly accepted a copy of the entire New Testament. Many studied it eagerly. They wanted to know more about this wonderful Savior.

The missionaries came away from these meetings so encouraged that they did not even mind how late it was. Often midnight had come and long gone before they got back to their station.

In early 1944 the French troops at Fort Archambault received orders to join General LeClerc's army. Several who attended the Saturday meeting were under deep conviction. One fellow especially struggled within himself, having been studying for the priesthood before he was forced to leave France.

"If I could only believe that the Bible is truly God's Word," he stated, clenching a fist as he spoke to Paul before marching off, "I would not hesitate a moment to accept its message of salvation."

"Well, son, it's up to you. You know the way of salvation, but you'll just have to decide whether to accept it or not. We'll pray for you."

The soldier said a reluctant good-bye to Metzlers and joined his company. Paul and Etiennette waved until there were only specks in the distance. They felt as if they were watching their own sons head into the jaws of lions.

"Paul," called Etiennette just a few days later, "our first letter from one of 'our boys.' It was sent from Fort Lamy."

". . . My doubts are finished," wrote the former student priest. "I am now happy in the knowledge that the Lord has saved me. . . ."

Paul and Etiennette rejoiced with the angelic choirs!

Later letters reported that as LeClerc's army snaked their way through the Sahara Desert and into Tunisia, "Metzler's boys" still held their gospel meetings. Each Saturday when they drove their trucks into the nightly wagon-train circle, they would sing the songs they had learned and read the Word. They wished Monsieur Metzler could be with them to explain more of it.

LeClerc's troops eventually joined a multinational force to invade Normandy in June of 1944. The missionaries prayed and listened to the radio for news of the assault.

Etiennette recognized the handwriting on the envelope and tore it open.

"Paul, it is from one of the boys," she called.

She read aloud for a few lines before her voice trailed off. She just stared at the page. Paul took the letter from her and read silently.

"What is it?" Mary asked.

"D day," Paul answered hoarsely.

"They were all killed," Etiennette managed.

"All except one." Paul let the letter flutter to the table.

"Well, now we know why the Lord worked so many miracles to get us back to Africa when He did," Mary quietly broke into their thoughts. "At least a number of the boys are in Heaven today."

* * *

While their parents spent time teaching Africans and French and English soldiers, Jack and Evelyne spent time playing with the baby mongoose a friend had given them. The mongoose belonged to each of them in turn on alternate days, by decree of a wise mother.

One day the family drove to an outstation for a service. They took the beloved pet with them as usual. On the return trip, Paul saw a flock of guinea fowl and could not resist stopping to bag a few. Jack wanted to tag along, so left instructions with Evelyne to baby-sit "his" mongoose.

"Take good care of him, Evelyne. We won't be long."

She nodded. She "owned" the pet all day yesterday and would again all day tomorrow, but now she could have some of Jack's day too! Not a bad deal. She sat proudly in the backseat with her charge, wondering if the African women walking along the road could see what a good job she was doing.

Suddenly the creature bounded out a car door that had not been closed securely.

"Oh no!" Evelyne squealed and bounded after him.

He raced for open country on the other side of the road, but one of the women intercepted him and whacked him over the head with her walking stick. Then she picked him up and walked over to ask the horrified Etiennette if she would like to buy him. Evelyne burst into tears. Their beloved pet was gone for good and she had been in charge. What would Jack say?

Shortly after the African women had walked off with their prize, Paul and Jack showed up with their guinea fowl. Jack started rattling off his exploits when he noticed Evelyne's tears. His eyes scanned the backseat. No mongoose. His heart skipped a beat.

"What's the matter? Where is he?"

The boy held his breath. His eyes filled with tears as Evelyne choked out the story.

"All I want to know is," he sobbed, "did he suffer?"

"No." Etiennette put an arm around him. "It was quick and painless."

"But we can't bury him," Evelyne wailed.

The thought brought fresh tears to Jack's eyes. For years the Metzler children had buried their pets in the special little graveyard at the mission station. Solemn funeral services had been held for a monkey who drank some kerosene out of a bottle, a Siamese cat who slept beneath the wheels of a car and birds too numerous to mention. Losing their pet mongoose was bad enough, but now they could not even give him a special place with the others or put his name on a stick.

In their small world the youngsters grieved, while across the free world adults mourned their own losses and prayed for a quick victory for the Allies. The Normandy invasion had slowly pushed the Germans back, liberating Paris two and a half months later. Finally, in December of 1944, the Allies crushed Germany's last desperate counterattack. It was the beginning of the end.

While the Axis armies crumbled and the Yalta Conference divided the postwar world, Edwin Metzler quietly turned sixteen. Paul and Etiennette had lost spiritual sons in the war, but God had allowed the fighting to end before their physical son had to go.

By the time of the Potsdam Conference in midsummer, life in Balimba had settled down to a more normal pace, and the rest of the soldiers from Fort Archambault went home. Rationing ended, and travel abroad became safer. Hélène and Rachel wrote from the United States to announce that Baptist Bible Seminary of Johnson City, New York (now Baptist Bible College and Seminary, Clarks Summit, Pennsylvania) had accepted them for the fall term. Life sprouted promise like a late spring after a long, hard winter.

In 1946, the Metzlers returned to the United States on furlough to spend the school year with their younger children in Mishawaka. More members of the family came together for a longer time this year than they had since 1940. What a treat!

Of course, the missionaries also reported to their supporting churches during this furlough. One trip took Paul to the 31st Street Baptist Church in Indianapolis, Indiana.

"And you haven't bothered to get your back X-rayed?" Pastor Robert McCarthy demanded when he heard how the car had fallen on Paul in 1938. "How can you neglect God's temple so? You must go get X rays at the hospital in town. It's been nearly eight years, Rev. Metzler! No telling what kind of damage has been done."

"I guess I never thought about X rays," Paul shrugged. "God always took care of me. But you're right. I'll get an appointment."

Pastor McCarthy accompanied Paul when he went to the orthopedic surgeon to get the results of the X rays.

"If you're telling the truth about how long ago this accident occurred," the surgeon said, shaking his head, "this X ray makes us doctors liars. We would say that it is impossible that one with this injury should still be alive and going as you are."

He swept his hand across the film to illustrate what he said next.

"It shows that you have three distinct lesions of the spine with several crushed vertebrae. We strongly advise immediate surgery, for the condition will deteriorate if left as it is."

A few days later Paul checked into the hospital. Surgeons took bone from both of his shins for spinal bone grafts to correct two of the lesions. The third would have to be done another time. Flat on his back in a body cast, Paul recuperated in the hospital for fifty days.

"The first time in six years my family gets some time together and I'm stuck here," he grumbled to himself. He deliberately set his mind on the Lord to conquer his discontented spirit, and memories of God's blessings on his family filled his thoughts.

Two daughters in seminary and a son nearly in college, he mused. I must be getting old. He chuckled to himself. Thank You, God.

When it came time to return to the field in 1947, Paul and Etiennette knew their children would be fine. Hélène and Rachel were still in seminary in New York. Edwin would finish high school while taking some college courses at John Brown University in Arkansas. Ralph, Jack and Evelyne attended the military academy at John Brown. Paul's brother Lawrence and his wife had agreed to take the youngest two when they began high school in a few years. Satisfied with these arrangements, the missionaries traveled back to Chad for another term.

The Balimba station surely looked good. A longtime friend had left word for them to visit him as soon as possible, so Paul and Etiennette drove the eight miles first thing. Monsieur Tiran had discovered a thief several days before and sustained a machete wound that refused to heal properly.

"We'll say it again and again, but you must ask forgiveness for your sin and accept Christ as your Savior," Paul urged, concerned over his friend's rapidly failing health. "No amount of money or position can get you to Heaven. Stop trusting yourself and start trusting the Son of God before it's too late. The only hard part is putting aside your own pride."

Paul grabbed his Bible and flipped to the back.

"Listen to Revelation 3:20."

He ran his finger down the page until he found it. " 'Behold, I stand at the door, and knock: if any man hear my voice, and open the door, I will come in to him, and will sup with him, and he with me.' Let Jesus come in now."

Tears slipped out from behind the patient's closed eyelids.

"Yes, I am ready now," he said. "God has been knocking a long time at my door."

Monsieur Tiran sighed heavily.

"He began back in 1938 that day in the cemetery at Lilianne's funeral and has been knocking ever since."

He opened his moist eyes to look at his friends.

"Perhaps you wondered why I did not shake hands with you that day."

His breathing was becoming more labored.

"I did not want to see anyone."

He paused to catch his breath.

"I went directly home from the cemetery."

He coughed and struggled to get his breath. Paul and Etiennette stayed only long enough to be sure their friend had indeed accepted the Lord as Savior, then left him to rest. A few days later he slipped into eternity with his new Friend. Lilianne's death had certainly not been caused by an unjust God as Monsieur Tiran had once thought, but had been allowed by a loving God Who let a child minister to many. That was spiritual victory.

A personal victory for Paul and Etiennette came with a letter from Hélène in June 1948, announcing her graduation from seminary and acceptance to nursing school. Rachel planned to take an extra year of studies, she added, but both planned to return to Chad as missionaries. The parents thanked God for His guidance, praising Him that their children were serving Him.

Doctor's orders brought the Metzlers back to the States in the fall. Paul simply had to slow down. This time they settled in Binghamton, New York, so Paul could teach missions at Baptist Bible Seminary. He took courses as well, in order to earn the diploma he had worked toward many years ago at Moody Bible Institute in Chicago. He looked forward to graduating in the spring with Rachel.

That Christmas Hélène came the sixty miles from her nursing school, and the younger four journeyed from Arkansas. Each savored every moment of this holiday together. They thanked God for this special Christmas gift.

In May of 1949, two Metzlers, father and daughter, graduated from BBS. Rachel began candidacy proceedings with Baptist Mid-Missions, her parents' board. Paul and Etiennette traveled back to Indiana to see the doctor about Paul's back. Edwin transferred to Calvin College in Grand Rapids, Michigan, with his dad's help. Ralph graduated from high school in June and settled in Mishawaka, Indiana, to look for work. Jack and Evelyne moved in with their aunt and uncle in Arizona.

"Of course we'll have to operate to correct the remaining lesion," the doctor said. "The other bone grafts are doing fine, so now's the time to get this last one done."

He leveled a finger at his patient.

"Don't you dare put it off any longer."

"All right, you win," Paul threw up his hands in mock surrender. "That's what my wife says, too, and a pastor friend of mine. I'm outnumbered."

He checked into Riley's Hospital in Indianapolis, and this time bone from the hip did the trick. The missionary used his prolonged recovery period to tell several Christian student nurses how much they were needed on the mission field. Some determined to go into missionary service when they graduated.

CHAPTER
22

**Paul witnesses while in the hospital
again. Metzlers go to Haiti
to establish a work there.**

While recuperating in the hospital after this last surgery, Paul grabbed opportunities to testify of God's grace to the unsaved patients around him. He started work in his new mission field his first evening on the ward, after the world came out of the fog. A visitor headed off the ward in tears.

"Ma'am," Paul called. "What's the matter? May I help you?"

She hesitated, but took the few steps over, shaking her head hopelessly.

"They are going to have to amputate my husband's leg tomorrow morning," she sobbed.

"I don't know whether you believe in prayer or not, but I do," he said soothingly, "and I want you to tell your husband that I'll be praying for him as he goes to the operating room tomorrow."

The woman smiled her thanks through her tears and turned back to tell her husband. The next morning he raised his head from his stretcher as he passed Paul's bed on the way to surgery.

"I'm counting on you, Buddy," he called out.

Paul pieced the story together. The fellow had just been brought in the day before after bumping a high tension line with his ladder, his wife said. More than three thousand volts burned into his left hand and finally burned out through his left foot, the orderly added, shaking his head. A friend who came to comfort the wife said that the electricity had been so powerful that it fused together the metal buckles on the poor fellow's galoshes.

No wonder they had to amputate. Paul prayed for skill for the surgeons and for quick recovery, but especially for peace for the couple.

The peace did not seem to be coming as he recovered. The amputee swore at the nurses when they would not give him everything he wanted. Although his bed was too far from Paul's to converse, the missionary did send notes via the nurses to try to comfort him.

One day Paul was finally allowed up in a wheelchair. As he sat savoring this step of progress in his condition, he noticed the amputee weeping uncontrollably into his pillow. Paul painstakingly made his way across the ward.

"My friend, what's the matter?"

After a moment the muffled sobs slowed and the heaving shoulders calmed a bit. Slowly the tear-stained face rose from the security of the pillow. A long sigh deflated his body.

"Tomorrow the butchers are going to amputate my arm."

His utter hopelessness stung Paul's heart.

"As if that's not enough," the amputee continued, "a nurse just told me that they just admitted my wife as a patient too. My children have been sent to a relative in Kentucky."

"Brother, you certainly need a friend now," the missionary said as he edged closer. "You need to be sure that God is on your side. If you knew Him, you could tell Him about these problems and He would help you."

The amputee closed his eyes, let his shoulders droop and heaved another long sigh as he sank back into his pillows. Paul prayed silently. After a few minutes his companion propped his head back up and partially turned.

"A long time ago I accepted Christ as my Savior, but I drifted away from Him and have lived an awful life. I don't think the Lord will want to do anything for me now."

Paul smiled.

"You know, I believe that Matthew 11:28 was written with you in mind. It says, 'Come unto me, all ye that labour and are heavy laden, and I will give you rest.' "

He laid his arm as far around the prodigal's shoulder as he could reach and prayed with him. Haltingly, this backslidden Christian confessed his sins to God and asked forgiveness.

"What's happened to that man?" the nurses whispered to each other the next day. "We haven't heard one word of cursing from him all day. Is he that ill?"

Finally Paul's doctor said he could leave the hospital. He bade farewell from bed to bed to each one with whom he had talked and prayed. The double amputee vigorously waved Paul over, his eyes shining.

"Perhaps you wonder why you had to leave Africa and come all the way here to have this operation," he began eagerly. "You may even be wondering why that car fell on your back in 1938."

He tapped his chest confidently.

"I can tell you why. God wanted you here when I came. I was running from God and desperate when you came to me. I'd decided that as soon as I left the hospital I'd commit suicide. But now everything has changed."

He flung out his right arm to emphasize his point.

"And just today I heard that my boss down at the state power company can give me a job for the rest of my life as a watchman. My wife's out of the hospital, and I'll be going home soon. Praise the Lord!"

From long experience Paul did recognize that God had been in charge during his own accident eleven years ago and during this man's accident now. He knew God plans events and times them just right for

His specific purpose. What a comfort to serve such a great God.

"You might as well get used to that back brace," the doctor told Paul before letting him go on home. "You'll be wearing that thing a long time. And remember, your back won't heal if you don't rest." With a smile he added, "You're not getting any younger, you know."

The doctor did not need to worry. Constant pain prevented strenuous activity. Besides, the brace made movement awkward. Paul and Etiennette were adapting to his restrictions when Baptist Mid-Missions contacted them.

"Mr. and Mrs. Ferrazzini have been our only missionaries in Haiti for years," the representative told them. "But now they're on emergency health leave and may never be able to return. Of course they couldn't take time to pack everything, so they need someone to send their belongings to them in Switzerland. They want to sign the property over to the Mission, too, and the deacons there in Jacmel are begging for help. We do have another couple heading out, but it'll be some months yet before they can go. You two fit all the requirements. Will you go?"

The veteran missionaries prayed about it.

"Yes, we'll be glad to go," they notified the home office. "Of course we expect our Lord to take us back to Chad one day, but we can help in the Caribbean for now."

They hurried through the preparations. Then, shortly before leaving for Haiti, Paul lost his balance and toppled over.

"Ugh!"

The wind had been knocked out of him. Hands reached down to help him up.

"I'll be just fine, thanks," he insisted when back on his feet.

"Paul, maybe we should not go to Haiti until we are sure your fall has not damaged your back again," Etiennette cautioned. "Maybe a few weeks of rest will do it, and we could still go out and help the Christians in Jacmel."

"Aw, I said I'll be just fine," he emphasized with a wave of his hand. "Stop worrying."

Be grateful she is concerned for you, Paul's heart scolded him. His independence softened, and he smiled over at his wife.

"The Lord will keep me going as long as He wants us there," he said.

He and Etiennette flew on schedule out of Miami to Port-au-Prince, the capital of Haiti.

"How do we get to Jacmel?" they asked.

"Well, you can drive," came the reply, "but the road is not good.

It goes through the mountains and takes six hours."

Paul shook his head. Etiennette was right. He really should take some precautions when he could.

"I've just had back surgery. I can't do that. How about flying?"

"Oh yes, that is the best way. It takes just twenty minutes."

One of the deacons picked them up when they landed.

"Is there a boardinghouse nearby where we can stay?" they asked as they threw their baggage into the truck.

"A boardinghouse?" the deacon repeated in surprise. "You can stay in the house on mission property."

"Well, yes, thank you, but we know it has not been lived in for some time now," Etiennette explained. "We cannot waste time cleaning and fixing it up when there is so much to do in the work here."

"But the house will not cost you rent," the deacon urged, not paying much attention to his driving. "And it is right near the church."

"We certainly appreciate your concern," Paul spoke up, "but my wife's right. We really do need to find a good boardinghouse."

They quickly located one and settled in. There was so much to do. Where should they begin? The man who had tried to fill in as pastor needed more training, and other churches in the surrounding country needed to be visited. The mission property needed to be deeded and registered in the Mission's name, and the Ferrazzinis' belongings needed to be packed and sent. The veteran missionaries rolled up their sleeves and went to work.

"And how far is the church today?" Paul asked the deacon with him.

"Oh, this one is just over that pass," he answered, pointing to a mountain across town.

Paul scanned the rocky landscape and groaned.

Lord, please give me strength, he prayed silently as he mounted his mule. The path wound steeply up and then dropped behind the ridge. Knives seemed to be stabbing him in the back. Why did his mule have to find all the bumps? Well, at least they did not have to walk this time. That hurt worse.

After several such trips Paul knew he could not stay any longer. Only fervent prayer had gotten him through those visits to outlying churches, and now he just had to get more medical help for his back. What a hard decision to have to make. He and Etiennette had finished the specific tasks they had set out to do, but many needs remained, and the new missionaries had many adjustments to make. The veteran missionaries hated to go just yet but knew they would have to leave just as soon as the new missionaries arrived.

Many Haitian believers escorted Paul and Etiennette to the airport. Good-bye tears betrayed the strong ties that had developed in those four short months. As the plane took off for the United States, the veteran missionaries prayed for more young people to come work in this fertile field.

* * *

The Metzlers returned to the Chad as soon as Paul was able. It felt good to be back. Far away from their children, they did not feel cut off because of the letters going back and forth.

Ralph had been having trouble finding a job in Mishawaka because he was eligible for the draft. No company would hire someone they knew could be swept away for military duty at any time, and for whom they would have to keep a job with its normal seniority and benefits. In desperation, he had tried to enlist but had been rejected. Part of two fingers of his left hand were missing as a result of a hunting accident. Armed with the rejection papers and his Uncle D. J.'s recommendation, Ralph returned to Bendix, where his dad had worked many years before, and was finally hired.

Jack and Evelyne wrote from Arizona, sending love from Uncle Lawrence and Aunt Hildy. The Lord was bringing in Rachel's support, another letter said, and she would be out with the folks before the end of 1950.

Hélène had another year of nursing school before she could come. She wrote that she had become good friends with Lois Harshman, another student nurse interested in the Chad, who also lived in Mishawaka. Hélène added that Edwin had met Lois at First Baptist Church while visiting Grandma Metzler, and suddenly he began visiting Grandma more and more often. Finally Edwin wrote that he wanted to get married after Lois graduated in the fall.

In 1951 Baptist Mid-Missions accepted Hélène for missionary service in Chad, and she began deputation. Ralph was drafted after all and went off to basic training. His tour would be over in two years, and he would return to Mishawaka with a new wife and settle down to his job at Bendix.

Edwin continued at Calvin College and at his job while his new wife enrolled in Grand Rapids Baptist College and found a full-time job at Blodgett Memorial Hospital. They graduated in 1952 and moved to Binghamton, New York, to attend Baptist Bible Seminary. That year the former Mary Kneeland, the missionary nurse who had worked with Metzlers in Chad, visited the young couple. Edwin and Lois could hardly wait to see her and her husband, Roy G. Hamman. She had married him after the death of his first wife, and then continued to serve with him in Chad.

"Remember, Aunt Mary, when you were housemother for Ralph and me at school in Fort Crampel?"

"Do I ever!" "Aunt" Mary rolled her eyes and laughed.

"And I'll never forget when you made a splint out of an orange crate for my knee. I'd cut it clear to the bone. What was it—a half bottle of iodine you used?"

"Yes, about half a pint. And I used a needle and thread out of the sewing kit to sew it up."

"You were creative too," Edwin chuckled. "I now have my initial on my knee."

Edwin paused and grew more serious.

"You helped me through spiritual crises too. Remember, I was saved in 1938."

"Yes, I remember," Aunt Mary smiled. "And that was the year the car fell on your father and that Lilianne died. The Lord gave you spiritual life, saved your father's life and let Lilianne start her heavenly life. All in one year!"

"I never thought of it like that before," Edwin replied slowly. "Sometimes hindsight makes it easier to see God working."

Then he brightened.

"Speaking of God working, have you heard that we're headed back to Chad as missionaries?"

He grinned at Lois.

"Great!" Aunt Mary and Uncle Roy encouraged them. "We look forward to working with you."

"By the way, did you hear that Father recently hurt his back again?"

"No, what happened?"

"He was working on a church roof when his back gave out. His guardian angels caught him, but he's in a lot of pain again."

CHAPTER
23

Recruiting new missionaries is urgent; then Metzlers go to France as missionaries.

Paul and Etiennette had to return to the United States in 1952 because of Paul's back. From their home in Ceres, California, they served as West Coast Mission representatives to churches in California, Oregon, Washington, Idaho and Arizona. Two goals drove them on: to recruit young people who would gather in the spiritual harvest and to raise money to send them.

While returning from Washington State one winter's evening, Paul recognized the Lord's urging to stop for the night. He had spent the entire day driving through cold, miserable rain.

"But Lord," he argued aloud, "there are only about two hundred miles left to get home. If I keep on driving, I can probably arrive by midnight."

The Lord put distinct thoughts in his tired mind. You must cross the Siskiyou Mountain to get home, and just listen to the rain. It has turned to sleet. Icy mountain roads are dangerous in daylight, but more so in the darkness. You had better stop.

The windshield wipers beat their rhythm, clearing glimpses through the wet darkness ahead. A light drew closer with each glimpse. A sign. Just a few more swipes of the wipers and maybe I can see what it says, Paul told himself. He strained to read, "Last Chance Motel."

He pulled into the parking lot and sighed. But I do not have the money, part of him said. What good is money if you slide off the mountain and are never heard from again? the other part of him countered. Besides, it is cold. But a hot cup of coffee would warm me up just as well as a cabin and cost a lot less. Well, it could not hurt to see how much it really would cost. It might be nice and warm inside the office, and I could stretch my legs, he decided. Maybe there are no open cabins anyway.

"Just one left, sir, and a double," the owner said. "Will cost you twelve dollars."

Paul's eyebrows jumped into his hairline.

"Twelve dollars!"

"But Mister," the owner warned, "you'd better not try that mountain tonight."

Paul sighed.

"Well, in Philippians 4:19 God promises to supply all my needs," he said as he reached for his wallet. "I'll take it."

As soon as he had brought in his suitcase, he turned the heat all the way up and wrapped himself in every blanket he could find. The cold dampness cut clear to the bone. Exhaustion overtook him, but the howling storm outside woke him up several times that night.

The next morning the motel owner invited Paul over for a cup of coffee before he pulled out.

"Have a set of chains?" the owner asked.

"Yes, why?"

"Better put them on. I live here. I know."

Paul did put his chains on before leaving, and thanked God for the advice every time he drove up a treacherous incline or negotiated an icy curve. During the night at least a dozen cars had plunged hundreds of feet into the ravine, and every few miles a wrecker struggled to pull cars out of hopeless positions along the road. Several people had frozen to death.

Last Chance, the missionary mused. What an appropriate name for that motel. Many times I have presented Christ as the last chance and the only chance, but so many have refused to listen and have gone over the precipice into a Christless eternity or left themselves helpless and frozen in sin. He shook his head. "Thank You, Lord, for saving me," he whispered.

In 1953 Paul became deputation secretary for Baptist Mid-Missions and worked out of the home office in Cleveland, Ohio. He grabbed opportunities for missionary conferences in churches throughout the country. He loved to see young people dedicate their lives to the Lord's work, and he loved to see others give willingly to send them.

There seemed no end to the desperate needs on so many fields. Paul and Etiennette began to think they would be more useful to the Lord filling some of these needs rather than just telling others about them. Then several missionaries in French Equatorial Africa signed a letter thanking the Rev. Metzler for his faithful field presentations over the years. They said that God had led each of them into missions because of his efforts.

Nothing could have encouraged Paul and Etiennette more. Now they were able to see that more needs could be met by recruiting many missionaries than by their returning to the mission field with Paul's bad back. The deputation secretary redoubled his efforts.

When the opportunity came to work in France, however, Paul and Etiennette jumped at it. Paul's back could not handle rough African roads, but Europe had paved roads. Besides, with his back brace he had managed so far on American roads. It felt mighty good to be on the way to work in the field once more.

Shortly after they arrived in France, a Mission representative contacted Paul and Etiennette.

"Our greatest need right now is at Bordeaux," he said. "We just started a work there, and we need someone who knows how to organize it. Also, there is an opportunity to work with the military. You already know how to do that, so could you get things off the ground?"

After praying about it, Paul and Etiennette decided to accept. They rented a house with a large dining room and parlor and started inviting United States Army and Air Force personnel over for games, fellowship and Bible studies. Many soldiers brought their wives and children along to the fellowships to help combat their homesickness. Etiennette invited French young people over, too, and soon friendships blossomed. Many dug deeper into God's Word and grew stronger in their faith.

At first Paul worked in cooperation with the chaplains to minister to the hundreds stationed at Bordeaux, La Pallice, Mérignac and Poitiers. Then, when offered the positions himself, he accepted. He regularly invited a few at a time over for a home-cooked meal throughout the six years he and Etiennette served in France. Some even kept in touch after they returned to the States. At least these boys would not all march off to their deaths.

Paul did not forget his responsibilities to civilians even when so immersed in the soldiers' lives. He held regular services in a downtown chapel and helped open the Baptist Bible Institute of Bordeaux on property that could be adapted for summer camp. Children and young people came from miles around, and many made decisions for Christ.

Several graduates of the Baptist Bible Institute are still serving the Lord as teachers throughout Europe. Victor Rodriguez, on the other hand, is pastor of a Baptist church in Dijon, France. Roger Reisacher took seminary training in the United States, served as a missionary in Chad and is presently back in France as a missionary under Baptist Mid-Missions.

During all this time Paul and Etiennette could hardly keep up with their children's changing lives. Rachel furloughed in the States while Hélène kept the dispensary open in Chad. Edwin and Lois had been accepted by Baptist Mid-Missions in 1954, and were starting deputation for Chad with dental training in Kentucky. Jack had graduated from high school and settled in Mishawaka, marrying within a few years. He and Ralph spent much free time hunting with bow and arrow as Saria had taught them many years before.

Then it was Hélène's turn to take a furlough while Rachel kept the station going. Hélène wanted to teach Chadians how to be midwives and nurses, so she squeezed in a midwifery course in New York between meetings. Evelyne had also graduated from high school and was attending Baptist Bible Seminary to prepare for missionary work in Chad.

"Now Edwin," Hélène and Rachel wrote him during his deputation, "be sure France officially recognizes your citizenship before you go traipsing off to Chad. It's still in French Equatorial Africa, you know."

"Aw, they already know I'm an American. Remember all those papers I filled out when I was eighteen? Well, there had to be enough of them for every colonial official to get a copy," he chuckled, "and they clearly said that I chose my United States citizenship over my French citizenship."

He chuckled again.

"Isn't it terrible how governments make you choose between your own mother and father?"

"The colonial officials may not have such a great sense of humor," his sisters warned. "We know ministerial students aren't drafted in the United States, but France is not so picky."

"Well, all right, I'll check it out," he conceded. "I wouldn't look good in a Foreign Legion uniform anyway."

A Mission representative accompanied Edwin to Washington, D.C., to try to straighten out the legal tangle.

"Yes," the authorities responded, "Edwin should have reconfirmed his citizenship six months before his twenty-first birthday. Unfortunately, if he returns now, he will be drafted immediately. We regret that no one told him, but that is the law."

Edwin wrote his parents to please check further for him since they knew just whom to contact in Brazzaville, the capital of French Equatorial Africa.

"Let Edwin come on over," authorities in Brazzaville replied. "We do not think his dual citizenship will become a problem."

"They mean well, but don't be fooled," Hélène and Rachel insisted. "We know of another case like yours. That fellow really did get sent to the front lines when he came back to French soil. Remember, France is fighting to keep its colonies, so there still are front lines to be sent to."

With three-fourths of their support already pledged, Edwin and Lois had to decide on another field. The Mission proposed two other African countries that desperately needed help. After much prayer they chose Liberia on the west coast of Africa. In 1956 they sailed with their little daughter.

In Bordeaux Paul once again had to seek medical care for his aching back.

"It is arthritis, Monsieur," the doctor told him. "It will continue creeping along your spine until you can no longer do your work in any cold, damp climate like this. Go where it is warm. That will do you as much good as anything I can do for you."

"Etiennette," Paul called as he walked in the house later. "The doctor wants us to move."

He chuckled at the surprise on her face when she came around the corner from the kitchen, wiping her hands on her apron.

"If we stay too long, you'll have to buy me a cane," he teased.

"We will have to make arrangements for the work here," Etiennette thought aloud. "Who will take our place?"

"I've been praying about that all the way home," Paul replied, serious now. "We'll have to keep praying for a chaplain and a pastor downtown, but I think Dr. G. Millon will make a good director at the Institute."

Dr. Millon had started his career as a Roman Catholic missionary in Baghdad, Iraq. Like Luther and Calvin, however, he had been excommunicated in 1929 because he had discovered the Biblical teaching of the free grace of God and wanted to preach it. He went on to marry and serve as a pastor and then to spend eleven years as an evangelical missionary in North Africa. Later he became a professor in the Theological Seminary at Aix-en-Province, France.

Paul carefully explained to him that all the work of Baptist Mid-Missions is done on a faith basis, trusting God for the funds for salaries and operating expenses. However unused to these terms he was, Dr. Millon jumped at the chance to come teach God's Word in all its purity. For years afterward this former priest continued to write Bible courses and to teach in the Baptist Association of France.

CHAPTER
24

**Metzlers finally return to Chad and
help with translation work.**

P aul and Etiennette spent 1960 in Florida resting Paul's back and helping Evelyne with her deputation schedule as they could. They did get the chance to see some of their grandchildren, but had to scramble to see Edwin and Lois's three little girls before their furlough expired.

"Well, gentlemen, we'd like to go back to French Equa—er, I mean, the Republic of Chad," Paul told the Baptist Mid-Missions administrative committee in 1961.

He smiled over at his wife.

"We've been away about nine years now, and we sure miss it."

"What about your back trouble?" a concerned committee member asked.

"I'm doing fine with my back brace, and I hear the roads are a little better in Chad these days. Besides, the Lord will take care of me."

The committee deliberated a bit before responding.

"If you can get medical clearance from the orthopedic surgeon who did your surgery," they decided, "you may go with our blessing."

The surgeon insisted on extensive X rays and examinations.

"Rev. Metzler," he finally said, "there are indications of arthritis settling in, but I see no reason why you should not return to Africa. In fact, I recommend residence in a tropical climate."

Paul and Etiennette praised the Lord for that victory but had to keep praying about well-meant advice.

"Conditions are different from when you left," many warned. "You know Chad gained its independence from France last year. What if you're not even welcome anymore?"

"Well, you see, we're not going back because of the welcome we might receive," Paul smiled patiently, "but because the Lord is leading. The Lord will take care of us just as He took care of the apostle Paul when he went to Rome despite his friends' fears for him."

That October Paul and Etiennette headed for the airport in New York. They spent an hour there with Edwin and Lois and their girls who had just returned from the field on emergency health leave. Once on the airplane, Paul squirmed in his seat to get comfortable.

"Now, let's see," Etiennette murmured, counting on her fingers, "Hélène is home on furlough, Edwin just arrived, Ralph and Jack live in Mishawaka. Then there's Rachel and now Evelyne in Chad, and soon us."

She grinned over at Paul before snuggling in for a nap.

"Indiana claims half the Metzlers, and Chad gets the other half."

They finally landed at N'Djamena (formerly Fort Lamy), the capital of the Republic of Chad. It felt good to be home. The veteran missionaries eagerly took their place in line at the immigrations counter where a Chadian checked the passports instead of a Frenchman.

Paul pulled his passport out of his pocket. The agent took it absently, but suddenly his eyes lit up and he jerked up his head to be sure it was not a mistake. He thrust his hand through the opening in the screen separating them.

"So you have come back to us," he cried out. "We have been praying a long time."

After a short but joyous reunion despite the stares of the others in line, Paul and Etiennette boarded a small plane to go on to Sarh (formerly Fort Archambault).

"Remember our other inland trips by push-push?"

Paul settled back gratefully.

"Oh, yes, the good old days," Etiennette teased.

Before long they circled the airport at Sarh.

"Look at that!" Etiennette pointed out the window. "There is a whole crowd down there. What in the world can they be waiting for? There must be a dignitary on board."

Rachel and Evelyne rushed aboard as soon as the plane landed and escorted their parents off. Immediately beloved faces surrounded them. Scores of Christians from the area and pastors from churches in the bush had come to welcome them.

"You know, our well-meaning friends who warned us that things would be different were right," Paul chuckled. "We have never received such a warm welcome to a field before."

The next day was Sunday. Paul and Etiennette could hardly wait to go to church in Fort Archambault—Sarh—again.

"Why, the church is almost full already," Paul exclaimed as they arrived, "and we thought we'd be early."

"Look over there and over there," Etiennette waved a hand. "People are still coming. Two thousand auditorium seats will not be enough."

Everyone wanted to welcome Monsieur and Madame back personally, so it took Paul quite some time to make his way to the front. Three thousand five hundred pairs of ears perked up as he began his first Sango sermon in years. He stumbled a bit at first, but soon his message of God's grace flowed comfortably.

"The Lord's work has blossomed here," Rachel and Evelyne filled their parents in that afternoon. "Churches are multiplying, and we can see Christians growing."

They toured the dispensary Hélène had set up and the school

where both Rachel and Evelyne labored.

"Health and literacy seem to be slowly improving," Paul observed. "Looks like what Chad needs most of all at this point is a translation of the Bible."

"Yes, a Bible in Sara Madjingaye," Evelyne added.

"Sara?" Etiennette questioned. "What about Sango? We always use Sango because everyone speaks it to buy or sell anything."

"That's just it. Sango is everyone's language," Rachel explained. "Nationalistic feelings run strong nowadays, and Sara is emerging as the Chadian language."

Paul and Etiennette decided to join the committee of missionaries and national pastors working on a translation.

"We have finished several of the New Testament books," they reported, "but there is still a lot of work before we can print."*

In 1962 the Chadian government expanded its nationalism again. They passed a law requiring missionaries to form associations independent of any other African country and reserved the power to authorize them. Baptist Mid-Missions missionaries in the Republic of Chad and the Central African Republic (CAR) had always met in one field council. After all, they all used to be a part of French Equatorial Africa. Now they would have to create separate councils. Word spread to meet at Sarh.

"First they do not give us much notice," one missionary grumbled, "and then they choose the rainy season to make us all travel."

"If the penalty for noncompliance were not so drastic, I would have been quite tempted not to venture so far," another agreed.

Flooded roads hampered those coming from Koumra, and Bob Vaughn and Gene Bryant from Kyabe waded through deep water for many hours until they could get a canoe to finish the trip. Despite it all, the necessary association did take form, and the documents did manage to reach the proper hands by the deadline. Informally, however, the missionaries of Chad and the CAR continued to fellowship and to cooperate to some degree.

In 1965 Paul and Etiennette furloughed in the States. Edwin had settled in Mishawaka and was teaching school, and Ralph still worked at Bendix. Jack also lived there, but one year he fulfilled a dream and moved his wife and two daughters onto a homestead in Alaska. He purchased a bush plane and built a hunting lodge outside Anchorage. Hélène, Rachel and Evelyne still served as missionaries in Chad.

The graying missionaries boarded the airplane to return to Chad

---

*In 1972, copies of the New Testament could finally be distributed.

when the time came, still thinking about their children.

"I am thankful we learned early in our marriage to dedicate the children to the Lord," Etiennette remarked as she buckled her seat belt.

Paul wriggled a small pillow behind his lower back for comfort.

"Me too, but that didn't make everything peachy," he responded.

"No," sighed Etiennette, "and there are three small graves in Chad to prove it."

They sat a moment absorbed in thought. Paul finally broke the silence.

"But He did keep His Word to take care of us all these years."

"Yes, and that meant covering three continents to keep track of us," Etiennette grinned.

"That's right."

Paul held up three fingers and bent one over with the forefinger of his other hand.

"Let's see, Chad, that's in Africa—"

"Chadian churches," Etiennette interrupted to enumerate, "French and British soldiers, a school, a dispensary and Bible translation."

"Bordeaux in France, that's Europe—" Paul bent over another finger.

"Civilians and soldiers from countries all over Europe as well as the United States, and the Bible Institute," Etiennette cut in.

"And the United States as Mission representative," Paul added, bending over the remaining finger.

"Scores of young volunteers for mission service, and a burden for missions instilled in hundreds of hearts," Etiennette finished.

"Oh, and Haiti," Paul held up a fourth finger. "It was only a few months, but my back remembers."

He grinned at his wife.

"And the work was established on more solid ground," she added.

"And to think," Paul patted his wife's hand as they circled the Fort Archambault airport, "for forty-two years now our Lord has allowed us to be a part of it all."

"Surely His strength is manifested through our weakness."

CHAPTER
25

Hélène becomes ill and writes the first draft of this book. She dies before it is published. The Metzlers go to Washington, D.C., and meet the President.

Paul became a representative for Baptist Mid-Missions when he and Etiennette returned to the United States for good. They knew they could never again serve in a country with bumpy roads, rocky mountainsides or jungle paths. Paul's back just could not take it anymore. They did the next best thing, they felt, by telling of the needs so that others could go and give.

In 1966 Hélène flew back to the States on an emergency medical furlough. After her cancer surgery she came to live with them in the cottage by the lake in Sebring, Florida. Paul still had to keep up with his responsibilities in churches and conferences for the Mission, but parents and daughter treasured this special time together.

In November of 1967, Hélène died. Paul and Etiennette remembered how the Lord had given her back to them when she had been sick as a tiny baby, and how they had known He had a special plan for their firstborn. They rejoiced in her testimony throughout her life as well as the scores of medical personnel she came in contact with during her illness, and thanked God that she kept her eyes on life in Heaven instead of death on earth. But the house still felt empty.

The veteran missionaries continued to represent the Mission through that winter and on into the spring. They decided an apartment in town would take less work to keep up, leaving them plenty of time to visit churches and speak at conferences.

"Guess we're semi-retired," Paul winked at his wife as he re-checked their summer itinerary. "We've even had to lighten our schedule. We'll be traveling only sixteen thousand miles in five months this time."

They ended their trip with a stop at the Mission home office in Cleveland, Ohio, to pick up an engraved invitation. It read:

"The President and Mrs. Johnson request the pleasure of the company of the Reverend and Mrs. Paul Metzler at dinner on Wednesday evening, October 2, 1968, at eight o'clock."

The black-tie dinner was to be held in honor of the President of the Republic of Chad, His Excellency François Tombalbaye.

Etiennette blinked.

"This is Monday afternoon already."

She blinked again.

"We will have to get you a tuxedo, Paul, and I will need a formal with gloves, and I will have to get my hair done. . . ."

Her voice trailed off as she tried to digest everything the Mission's social secretary had told them.

"There's really nothing to be nervous about," Paul shrugged, his eyes twinkling. "After all, we're ambassadors for the King of Kings."

They drove down toward the capital. They would get a good night's rest at the Reverend Cooper's before tackling their shopping.

"That took no time at all," Etiennette said, smiling at Paul when they had rented his tuxedo. "Now," she turned to the saleslady, "do you have a formal that will match my brown shoes and clutch bag?"

The shop boasted scores of formal gowns but few the right size— and none acceptable.

"But that's the new style," their frustrated saleslady told them. "Everyone wears low-cut backs."

"These are not cut just a little low," Etiennette retorted, "they are cut almost to the waist. Besides, I do not care what everyone else wears. Maybe I should try another store."

"Let me look one more time," sighed the saleslady, sliding gown after gown down the rack. "Ah, here's one I didn't see before."

She pulled out the turquoise-blue crepe and held it up.

"It's more your style, and it's even your size."

Etiennette eyed the gown critically.

"Well, the sleeves are shorter than I would have liked, but it does have a back," she murmured.

Then she spoke up. "It is lovely. Now, I will need long gloves to match."

The gown cost only five dollars more to buy than to rent, so Etiennette bought it. She had been told to expect an invitation to a reception the evening following the dinner at the White House, so she was pleased that her purchase saved almost the entire cost of the second rental.

Etiennette kept her hair appointment at four o'clock Wednesday afternoon. Then she and Paul carefully dressed, and a friend drove them to the southwest gate of the White House shortly before eight o'clock. Policemen in dress uniform closed in from both sides and demanded to see their invitations. They peered in at the passengers; then, apparently satisfied, they told the driver which lane to take through the park to reach the proper door.

A crisp Marine offered Etiennette his arm to escort her inside. Paul followed them into the diplomatic receiving room where a Marine officer announced their arrival. An orchestra provided the background for starched military officers in black trousers and short white coats who shook their hands in welcome.

After a number of colonels, majors and admirals had introduced themselves, Etiennette began to recognize which branch of the service they represented by their adornments. Silver braids dangled from the shoulders of Navy officers, gold braids indicated the Army, and extra gold along the shoulder seam signified the Air Force.

She was trying to pick out Coast Guard officers when one of the waiters handed her a small envelope. The card inside told her to take her place at table number two when the time came for dinner. Paul's card directed him to table number eleven.

"How many tables are there?" they wondered aloud as they watched the room fill up.

"Enough to seat the one hundred and forty people who have been invited," one of the officers told them with a grin at their amazement.

All this visiting had made Etiennette thirsty, but she was not interested in the cocktails that waiters brought around on trays.

"Would it be possible to have ginger ale?" she asked.

The waiter did not answer, but one of the officers standing nearby heard her request and stepped in.

"Go and get some ginger ale," he ordered the waiter; then, turning to Etiennette, he said gallantly, "Ma'am, you may ask for whatever you please. If you'd like something before our man returns, there's orange juice on that tray over there."

Sure enough, she spied two glasses of orange juice among the wines and champagne.

"Oh, this is better yet. Thank you. Paul, would you like one?"

Then the lights brightened. President Tombalbaye and President and Mrs. Lyndon B. Johnson were announced.

Missionaries, officers and other dignitaries adjusted ties and gloves as they merged to file down the receiving line in alphabetical order. Before long Paul was shaking President Johnson's hand while one of the officers was introducing him and Etiennette. Then it was her turn.

"Good evening, Mr. President," she said as he smiled broadly at her.

Next in line stood the President of the Republic of Chad. Etiennette remembered François Tombalbaye when he had been a student in her school long ago, along with some of the other Chadian officials present.

"This is a real surprise," he said, raising his eyebrows. "Do you live around here?"

He must think we are neighbors of the Johnsons, Etiennette chuckled to herself.

She shook Mrs. Johnson's hand last. She is much prettier than her pictures, she thought, and quite a gracious hostess.

"I am so glad you can converse in French," Mrs. Johnson was saying, "as I cannot do that. I don't know one word."

When they left the receiving line, the couple followed those in front of them while the orchestra serenaded from the lobby. The dining room was alive with artistic flower arrangements. Candles adorned each table while a magnificent chandelier and elegant sconces along the walls added to the splendor. An officer helped them find which table bore their number, then each guest circled the table looking for the proper name tag.

Etiennette found herself seated beside His Excellency Georges Diguimbaye, minister of planning in Chad. He knew who she was, as he owned property in Balimba and knew most of the Christians there. On the other side of him sat a Supreme Court judge who also spoke French, and beyond him sat the wife of the mayor of Dallas, Texas. On Etiennette's other side sat a man who oversaw some of the television transmissions at the White House. Five others occupied the other chairs at the round table. Mrs. Johnson and President Tombalbaye smiled across from table number one.

Waiters finally began bringing out the first course. Etiennette watched as their attendant served the judge first, then the mayor's wife and then Etiennette herself. She forgot her puzzlement over this protocol as she tackled the delicacies served plate by plate. No bread, her Frenchwoman's mind noticed, but plenty of spoons and forks. She chuckled to herself.

Several guests smoked since cigarettes and matches were as plentiful as the nuts and candy at each table. The waiter turned two of Etiennette's glasses upside down when she waved away the wine, then filled one with ginger ale at her request. He left the champagne glass upright but empty.

During dessert Air Force violinists played their way into the dining room, ending their melodies only when President Johnson rose to give a speech. After the speech Etiennette turned to converse with His Excellency Diguimbaye and did not notice the waiter pour champagne into her glass.

"Do not mind that; it is just a form," the Chadian Minister assured her. "They are filling everyone's glasses."

The television man on Etiennette's other side drank his champagne before they rose to toast the President, so helped himself to some of hers. He drank that down as well after the toast, but Etiennette just set her glass back on the table.

Then it was President Tombalbaye's turn to give a speech, with official interpreters translating. Afterward the dinner party adjourned into another room for coffee where Etiennette and Paul gratefully found each other. Mrs. Johnson made her way over to them.

"I just wanted to tell you again how glad I am you're speaking

French to our Chadian guests," she said earnestly. "By the way, what faith are you?"

"We're Baptist," Paul answered.

"Oh really?" She seemed pleased. "Did you know that all Texas is Baptist? There are several Baptist preachers in the President's family."

She was swept away in the crowd before they could answer, so Metzlers turned to introduce themselves to the couple next to them. Both the Johnson daughters joined the ranks of new acquaintances Paul and Etiennette made that night. Mrs. Johnson appeared again as the missionaries chatted with President Tombalbaye.

"And how long were you in Africa, Mr. Metzler?" she asked.

"These are pioneers, Madame," the Chadian President answered for him. Then he added, wonder in his voice, "but they are both still in good health."

Paul chuckled.

"The Lord has taken care of us all these years."

"Did you know, Madame Johnson, that I had the honor of presenting Monsieur Metzler with a medal for distinguished public service to my country?" Tombalbaye put in.

"Is that right?"

Mrs. Johnson's eyebrows raised as she turned to Paul.

"Congratulations, Mr. Metzler. That's quite a distinction for a missionary."

"I was serving the Lord and had a chance to serve Chad in the process," Paul replied.

"It was not as large an affair as this," President Tombalbaye added, "but we made it impressive by Fort Archambault standards for all our award recipients."

"Oh, it was impressive," Paul exclaimed, grinning. "All those bigwigs of state and military officers sweating in their suits and dress uniforms while the Arabs sailed through the ceremony in their flowing robes."

They chuckled as they finished their coffee, and then the group split up as they followed the other guests into the music room where Robert Goulet and a jazz band provided entertainment.

"Ted and Lila!" Paul exclaimed, but the music drowned out his next words.

The two couples found a table as far away from the stage as they could, but still had to speak out to be heard.

"You must have received an invitation because you know some of the Chadians too," Paul tried again.

"Yes," nodded Ted and Lila Wimer, fellow Baptist Mid-Missions missionaries from Chad. "This has been a delightful evening until now," they called across the table.

"Yes, my head is pounding," Etiennette put in. "Let us go out to the lobby. I do not want another migraine."

They walked out to the lobby as several couples got up to dance. Etiennette asked a waiter for ginger ale again in place of the champagne that flowed freely. All four of them were growing tired, so shortly asked an officer if the President had gone to bed yet. The social secretary had told them this was the cue that the party was no longer so formal, and guests could go home whenever they chose. They learned that both presidents had left.

The exhausted missionaries gratefully left the storybook world. They had thoroughly enjoyed the evening until the piercing music at the end, but they were quite ready to go home now. The two couples walked through the park and out to the street corner to hail a taxi.

"Georges Diguimbaye feels there should be one big Protestant church in Chad," Etiennette said as they waited for a taxi to be available. "I tried to explain that that could never happen because our churches will cling to the Bible as our only authority no matter how the others are willing to compromise."

"Yes, and that divides people who want to add to Biblical revelation," Paul put in. "We'll have to keep praying that the gospel stays pure in Chad."

The couples had to wait a half hour before they could get a ride. Paul and Etiennette arrived back at their host's house after midnight, eager to drop into bed.

They rested the next day. President Tombalbaye had invited them to an informal reception that evening at the Mayflower Hotel, so Etiennette did not get to wear her White House gown again after all.

"Your girls are working very hard, and their pupils are doing very well," the Chadian President told Paul and Etiennette that night.

"America is a wonderful country," he added with enthusiasm. "This morning the Honorable Frank Carlson of the United States Senate gave me a prayer breakfast and asked me to pray. Just think of it," he gestured for emphasis, "in this country the Senate prays three times a week."

He shook his head incredulously.

"And to think they asked me to pray, and I prayed."

After the exceedingly ample smorgasbord, the missionaries chatted with other guests. Before they left, President Tombalbaye called for the photographer to take a picture of him with his former teacher and her husband.

CHAPTER
26

**Preaching in the Bahamas, Paul
becomes ill the last time.**

Paul and Etiennette returned home to Florida and the routine of representing the Mission when needed. Early in 1969 they were called to preach to Haitians stranded in the English-speaking Bahamas. As soon as they could, the couple flew out. Within the week Paul became ill but refused to return to the States for treatment.

"Someone has to explain God's Word to these refugees," he insisted. "They don't understand English."

"But Paul," Etiennette pleaded, "you are getting worse, and nobody here knows what is wrong. Please, let us go back to the States until you are better. Then we can come back here, and you can preach all you want."

"But there just aren't enough missionaries here who can preach in French," Paul argued. "What if some lost soul never hears God's plan of salvation because we leave? We're needed here for now."

"The Lord will send someone else if we ask Him," Etiennette tried again. "Please, let us go until you are better."

Not until he became too sick to preach did Paul consent to fly with Etiennette to West Palm Beach, Florida. By the time they landed, he could hardly breathe and had to be whisked off to the hospital.

"He just kept getting weaker," Etiennette explained to the doctor, "but he insisted on preaching the entire ten days. What is wrong?"

The doctor shrugged and shook his head.

"We don't know yet, Mrs. Metzler, but it doesn't look good. We've already started the regimen of tests, but it'll take a few days to get all the results in."

Etiennette stayed with friends near the hospital. Wanting the freedom to come and go without bothering anyone, the sixty-eight-year-old decided to learn to drive a car between her frequent visits to the hospital. She also took time to notify the children of their father's severe illness.

Edwin's family was able to come. Paul lay in his spotless hospital room smiling weakly at them, his white sheets pulled up to his shoulders. Tubes connected him to equipment by his bed.

"We hate to leave, Father," Edwin finally had to say, "but Lois and I have to be getting back to work soon. We'll be praying for you and Mother."

They left after the good-bye kisses, and that evening Paul slipped into a coma.

"I'm sorry, Mrs. Metzler," the doctor said. "He won't last the night. There's nothing we can do."

Etiennette sat all night with her beloved husband, praying for God's will and the grace to accept it. Then, at four o'clock Easter

Sunday morning, Paul opened his eyes again. Etiennette took his hand as God's peace flooded her heart.

"Bonjour, cheri," she greeted him quietly. "Today you will have the best Easter you have ever had. You will get to spend it in Heaven."

Paul brightened up.

"Praise the Lord!"

A few minutes later he slipped into his special Easter in the Lord's presence. Etiennette felt so empty, but there were telephone calls to make. She drew strength from the One Who had proved so faithful over the years.

Edwin, Ralph and Jack arranged to come to the funeral, but Rachel and Evelyne could not get in from Chad. Etiennette asked Dr. Roy G. Hamman to fly in from special meetings in California to preach the funeral message. He had been a fellow missionary in Chad and now served as pastor of Paul's home church in Mishawaka.

One whole side of the church filled with pastors from all over the United States. Roger Reisacher, a graduate of the Baptist Bible Institute of Bordeaux, France, took a few days off from seminary in Indiana, and caught a ride down with Edwin and Lois. He and many others seated in the pews realized how much they owed to the spiritual leadership of the man who no longer inhabited Paul Metzler's body.

They felt a loss, but knew that Paul would have said, "For to me to live is Christ, and to die is gain" (Phil. 1:21). Gain? How could death be gain? "Death is swallowed up in victory. O death, where is thy sting? O grave, where is thy victory? . . . But thanks be to God, [Who] giveth us the victory through our Lord Jesus Christ" (1 Cor. 15:54–57).

* * *

Sheldon B. Vance, United States ambassador to the Republic of Chad, sent condolences to Etiennette after he had "hastened to inform President Tombalbaye" of Paul's death. A little later President and Mrs. Johnson heard "through mutual friends of the sudden passing of" Paul and sent their "deepest sympathy."

Edwin and Ralph returned to the Mishawaka area after the funeral, and Jack to Alaska. Etiennette remained active in her church and maintained her ministries of prayer and personal letters of encouragement. She refused to let her own chronic back trouble keep her from driving herself wherever she wanted to go.

The end of Baptist Mid-Missions' triannual conference became a memorial service for Paul, recounting highlights of his forty-seven years as missionary-statesman. Missionaries from Chad and Central Africa sang a hymn Etiennette had translated into Sango. Then Dr.

Allan E. Lewis, president of Baptist Mid-Missions, closed the service asking God for the two requests Paul would have asked himself— blessings and protection for Etiennette and the family and more young people called out to labor for the Lord.

In 1973 Rachel and Evelyne started their ministry in Haiti, where they have remained. Etiennette moved into the retirement community of Maranatha Village in Sebring, Florida, in 1974, and still thoroughly enjoys it. Her neighbors include old friends like Mrs. Clarence Jeun- nette and Dr. Roy G. and Mary (Kneeland) Hamman. Periodically Etiennette has been able to visit her daughters in Haiti and to encourage believers there.

* * *

The Lord God took a boy who stuttered and made him a preaching force on three continents. He took a girl locked into one position in life and gave her great adventure. The work started so long ago by these two dedicated young people still thrives in the efforts of the one, and radiates through the lives of so many they have touched.

To God be the glory!